The Future of Professional Fields
Views from the Mexican Diaspora in Europe

By Red Global MX Europe

RED GLOBALMX
MEXICANOS CALIFICADOS
REGIÓN EUROPA

Published by *Red Global MX Europe*, Dublin, Ireland, www.rgmx.eu

Sold by: Amazon
Business & Economics > Careers > General
Business & Economics > Industries > General
ISBN-13: 978-1535551786
ISBN-10:153555178X

Dedicated to those Mexicans who have never really left.

You actively contribute to building the future of Mexico from your own corner of the world.

Index

Acknowledgements

The Editors wish to thank...

Each of the authors who have contributed to this project, turning dream into reality. Thank you for your enthusiastic response and professionalism.

Virginia Romero for challenging us with the possibility of writing this book in the first place.

Zahaira González for your talented contribution with the cover art.

Carolina Islas for your contribution not only as an author but for your dedicated work in editing and liaising with each author.

Ambassador of Mexico to the UK Diego Pickering, for your kind sponsorship, thank you!

Cynthia Vega, President of the Mexican Talent Network UK, for securing the seed capital for the printed version.

Eunice Rendón, Head of the Institute of Mexicans Abroad for writing the Foreword and contributing to strengthening Red Global MX.

Sofía Orozco for all your dedication and committed work for and on behalf of Red Global MX.

And a special thank you to *you*, the reader, for sharing this journey with us.

About Red Global MX

Red Global MX is a civic society effort that represents the Mexican diaspora which is decidedly connected to Mexico in a variety of non-profit endeavors. We are a network of Mexican professionals present in the Americas, Europe, and Asia who are actively engaged in development projects, in areas including science, technology, education, training, creative arts, culture, social responsibility, entrepreneurship and innovation, among others.

Over 8 thousand members, who are recognized in their fields, are organized through over 50 chapters scattered around the world.

Chapters collaborate with organizations in Mexico and in their host countries, in sectors spanning academia, the private sector, multilateral organizations and government entities.

Red Global MX is supported by the Mexican Ministry of Foreign Affairs (Institute of Mexicans Abroad) and by the network of Mexican Embassies and Consulates corresponding to each chapter.

Foreword

With almost one million and a half qualified Mexicans abroad, Mexico is the number one exporter of qualified diaspora in Latin America and the sixth worldwide. These are Mexican professionals who have succeeded in their fields abroad.

Supported by the Institute for Mexicans Abroad (IME), a special office of the Ministry of Foreign Affairs, a group of visionary and talented Mexicans living abroad created Red Global MX (RGMX).

In the context of our global knowledge economy, RGMX is a network and a platform that seeks to link efforts amongst qualified Mexicans residing overseas. The aim is to contribute to development projects in Mexico and in their host countries, i.e. their new homes.

From brain drain to talent circulation

The philosophy of Red Global turns the brain drain paradigm upside down, into talent circulation, representing a strategic potential advantage for our country, expanding its interests, cooperation and presence around the globe.

Red Global MX (RGMX)

The RGMX network has continued to grow and consolidate over time. Today there are 50 chapters in 23 countries. Members are role models not only in Mexico but in their local communities. They are private sector CEO's, Presidents and Directors, including business owners, in US, European and Asian chapters.

They also participate in international research and innovation projects as well as in art and social sciences initiatives in chapters including Ireland, New Zealand and China; or creative industries in Silicon Valley, Barcelona and France, among others.

Mexican *nodes*

Willing to connect the international advantages of knowledge transfer and networks, RGMX created the concept of a "node", which is a special type of chapter that sits *inside* Mexican territory. A Mexican node connects civil society, private sector, government and academy in order to work *glocally*: both globally *and* locally, with the support of the Mexican diaspora residing abroad but with direct local activities. This has kickstarted a variety of cooperation efforts, including the mentoring of high tech Mexican entrepreneurs by Mexican mentors living in Europe, for example.

About *The Future of Professional Fields*

This book serves as a showcase of the wide experience and vision of RGMX membership. It is a useful and valuable tool for our country and for other nations that wish to organize and empower their communities abroad.

It also serves as an example of the positive impact that the diaspora exerts when sharing their knowledge and experience. It documents the importance of joint efforts, between Mexicans abroad, but also within their host nations.

Through its pages and chapters, *The Future of Professional Fields* invites readers to reflect on the potential that qualified diasporas have for their home *and* host countries.

Mexican talent abroad

As a Mexican and as the director of the Institute for Mexicans Abroad, I am proud to have been asked to preface this book revealing Mexican talent. Their combined work is a testament to the significant role that Mexico continues to play globally in a diverse range of fields by virtue of the achievements of our nationals.

The great capacity, dynamism and willingness of Mexicans goes beyond borders to build meaningful networks; Red Global MX and this book are a perfect example of that.

Eunice Rendón, Ph.D.

Director, Institute of Mexicans Abroad
Mexico City
June 2016

Why this book?

SPARKING CURIOSITY

"I have a definition of success. For me, it's very simple… It's not about wealth and fame and power. It's about how many shining eyes I have around me." –Benjamin Sanders, The Art of Possibility.

As we were saying our goodbyes at the European Regional meeting in London in October 2015, Virginia Romero, member of the Swiss chapter threw a last minute challenge at all of us: What if this group wrote a book? But here's the thing: *what if's* can be dangerous! They may seem like innocent, innocuous questions, but let's not be fooled: they are powerful tools for instigating action. The risk—and great opportunity—lies in that instill a sense of possibility, that feeling that something may actually be *doable*.

At the time we were already overloaded with work from the conference, on top of our regular work load to even consider a project like this one: writing a book with twenty plus authors! Nevertheless, we decided to suspend reality for a moment and entertain the possibility: *what if we actually wrote a book?*

To make a long story short, less than nine months later this project has seen the light of day and is now in your hands.

A taste of our professional worlds

Explaining *why* a particular book is written can be complex. The short answer is that we, the authors and editors, wanted to share what we usually keep to ourselves professionally, giving a hint of what our (many times crazy) professional worlds look and feel like. We wanted to share the ideas that make us tick and which keep us engaged (or worried) in our day to day endeavors.

Links across the Atlantic with young talent

We also wrote this because we would like to spot trends and opportunities that may relevant to both our countries of residence and to our native Mexico, deepening the strategic links across the Atlantic with a focus on clusters that offer significant growth opportunities in the coming years.

But, perhaps most importantly, we wrote this book to contribute to the development of young talent in Mexico. We consider education (in both technical and non-technical areas) to be a key factor to the medium and long-term advancement of prosperity in our nation.

The Future of Professional Fields seeks to help ignite the thirst for more knowledge, helping uncover areas that may lead down a path of discovery and contribution.

Finally, in the true spirit of Red Global MX we encourage readers to reach out to the authors of this book, so that we may start a dialogue which we hope will lead to meaningful and fruitful collaboration.

Victor del Rosal

Coordinator, Red Global MX Europe

June 2016

1

The future of education in a world of white-collar automation

VICTOR DEL ROSAL, M.SC.*

Author of the book "Disruption: Emerging Technologies and the Future of Work", Founder of Emtechub, Lecturer at National College of Ireland, Dublin.

U p until the industrial revolution muscle power was limited to what animals and humans could provide. With the advent of the steam engine, the availability of physical power grew exponentially, marking an era of tremendous progress. This is referred to as the first machine age by Erik Brynjolfsson and Andrew Mcafee in their *Second Machine Age* book.

If muscle power was essential to that age, brain power is the key for the second machine age. However this is not the natural brain power of humans, but that afforded by computers. It is the era we live in, where plentiful computing power—which continues to grow exponentially—multiplies the availability of cognitive power. Today computers are doing the jobs that were reserved for humans not long ago. This is powering the era of automation.

Brynjolfsson and McAfee point out that it is the "exponential, digital, and combinatorial" nature of technology that underpins the powerful nature of the second machine age. Processes which were limited to human labor are now being performed by computer code. Automation will continue to especially impact work that is predictable and repetitive.

The implications are profound and far-reaching. Within two decades the equivalent of billions of new brains will be added to the global economy. But these will not be human brains but artificial intelligence agents performing all sorts of knowledge tasks.

Not so special after all

As the global supply in intelligence—human or artificial—increases, human cognition loses its value; it is no longer unique, especially as AI systems get more sophisticated. This is because the supply of computing power is steadily increasing, and it will do so until it becomes ubiquitous. Overall the price of a floating operation per second is dropping. All of this powers a cocktail of technologies that make us humans increasingly replaceable. Humans may not be so special after all. Computer code is replacing basic human cognitive functions across a variety of functions and industries.

One of the consequences of the technological progress is precisely our availability to replace human cognition with machine cognition.

Automation is not a new thing

However, automation is not a new thing. In a Pew Research Center study, Jim Warren, the founder and chair of the First Conference on Computers, Freedom & Privacy, wrote that "Automation has been replacing human labor—and demolishing jobs—for decades, and will continue to do so. It creates far fewer jobs than it destroys, and the jobs it does create often—probably usually—require far more education, knowledge, understanding and skills than the jobs it destroys."

Rex Troumbley, researcher at the University of Hawaii at Manoa, wrote, "We can expect robots, artificial intelligences, and other artilects to increasingly displace human labor, especially in wealthy parts of the world. We may see the emergence of a new economy not based upon wage labor and could be realizing the benefits of full unemployment (getting rid of the need to work in order to survive)".

The reason why this will start in wealthier parts of the world is simple: a worker in the developed world is more expensive than her peer in a developing country. There is simply more incentive for a corporation to start an automation process where wages are higher. In the developing world, where labor intensity is still affordable it will take longer, but it will also come of age.

AI and robotics will continue to displace low level worker skills

A top digital media strategist at a U.S. national public news organization responded, "Our continuing failure to re-train under-skilled workers will continue to create a glut of un- and underemployed as advances in AI and robotics require workers that are more educated than ever before. Those who attain those education levels will find new opportunities while under-skilled workers are left on the curb."

Rebecca Lieb, an industry analyst for the Altimeter Group and author, responded, "Enterprises will require a highly educated, digital and data literate workforce, which does not bode well for blue-collar workers, or softer skill white-collar workers. Given trends in U.S. education, this could lead to high demand for engineers from foreign countries (as we've seen in the past) with advanced degrees in engineering, mathematics, etc., as institutions of higher learning in this country fail to produce enough graduates with the requisite skill sets."

Education for the new wave of knowledge workers

If we accept that the new knowledge worker is an augmented human capable of leveraging knowledge and emerging technologies to achieve what a small army of non-augmented humans could do a few years ago, then we have to seriously ponder: how do you teach a learner like that?

No more carbon copies

In an Industrial economy, education was designed to replicate workers, so that they were interchangeable pieces of well-oiled machinery. However, exact copies of worker are no longer as useful or relevant, because, by virtue of automation we see that eventually most predictable patterns will be ultimately replaced. Emerging education must recognize that learners in the new economy are moving towards an era of specialization, where workers and entrepreneurs will be highly rewarded for coming up with unique solutions.

Education will then move away from the mass-production of graduates towards highly customized educational programs. Instead of following a cookie-cutter approach to teaching and learning we will realize that it makes more sense to follow highly personalized teaching-learning methodologies which are adapted to each learner. While technology will serve as a key enabler of this, the biggest challenge will not be technological or even methodological, but cultural. We need to reconsider the role of education for the era we have entered.

Realization of the student-worker-preneur

One of the questionable assumptions relates to how the educational system sees the learner: is she an employee? Is she an entrepreneur? Is she a perennial student?

John Baker, founder of Desire2Learn, asserts that "life in the industrial economy was typically viewed as a series of discrete segments: school, work and retirement. But this thinking is no longer viable as we have entered the era of lifelong learning."

Are we then teaching students to be employees and not entrepreneurs? While we may be tempted to answer that everyone must be trained as an entrepreneur, it does not mean that everyone wants to be *exclusively* one or the other. The reality might lie somewhere in between: we need for learners to become proactive lifelong learners, who will likely work for a company as a full-time employee at some stage, and will more-than-likely start their own company, or be a freelancer. Hence a more balanced term which reconciles reality and work trends might be summarized in the realization of the *student-worker-preneur*, a term I have coined to represent that each of us is a student who is a worker and an entrepreneur in different degrees throughout our careers.

Memory augmentation: commoditized knowledge

If, for all practical purposes, knowledge is a Google search away, memorizing things will become irrelevant. The idea of regurgitating dates and names for the sake of it will be seen as a waste of time. Access to information will become increasingly commoditized and it will also be enhanced and sophisticated: from voice commands, to augmented reality displays, to automatic face recognition—the trend in memory augmentation is clear: we will need to memorize less and less. This implies that as educators the emphasis should *not* be placed on getting students to remember and regurgitate data. The case is strengthened by the increasing volume and speed at which information is generated; the body of knowledge in any given profession can change not in a matter of years but months or weeks. Hence, knowing is not enough. The actual competence, doing, achieving something, is the real test.

Questioning the purpose of education

How can education keep up in times of exponential change?

Whereas in an Industrial age the quantity of graduates was the key variable to optimize, in the new economy, it will be the *quality* of graduates. Thus, instead of graduating professionals with the same (commoditized) skills, the most valuable education will be that which is able to cultivate the uniqueness of each learner, including an optimal mix of hard and soft skills, that is, technical and interpersonal competencies.

Learning to learn

Decades ago it used to be enough to learn a trade in a four or five-year university program. However today, by some estimates, half of the technical information that you learn in a university program might be outdated by the time you finish.

In an era where new industries and business models are born overnight, it is clear that being able to learn at a record speed will not only give the learner a competitive advantage but it will become an essential skill for life.

However, as explored, the limitation for this is no longer access to information. Nowadays anyone can learn virtually any trade online, thanks to Massively Open Online Courses (MOOC), or through full university courses made available by Universities including Harvard, Stanford, and the Massachusetts Institute of Technology. While certification is still closely held by universities, the actual knowledge to be learned has increasingly become commoditized. As the new currency is being able to do, and not just knowing, the ability to proactively engage in self-taught education that helps develop real world competencies will become paramount.

Raison d'être: the motivation to learn

Underlying the ability to learn is the motivation to learn. In an article by the Center for Teaching and Learning at Stanford University, author Barbara McCombs, director of the Human Motivation, Learning, and Development Center at the University of Denver, is quoted on seven qualities of students who are optimally motivated to learn. McCombs points out that optimally motivated students see schooling and education as personally relevant to their interests and goals; they believe that they possess the skills and competencies to successfully accomplish these learning goals; they see themselves as responsible agents in the definition and accomplishment of personal goals; they understand the higher level thinking and self-regulation skills that lead to goal attainment; they call into play processes for effectively and efficiently encoding, processing, and recalling information; they control emotions and moods that can facilitate or interfere with learning and motivation, and; they produce the performance outcomes that signal successful goal attainment.

From my own experience working with students and business clients over the years, I see a clear correlation between the *motivation* for learning and the ability to learn. I would argue that it is more important to have a *reason* for learning, a powerful *why* that inspires the learner to pursue education.

This can be tied back to the importance of solving problems. To paraphrase McCombs, learning can be enhanced when the learner sees that what they learn can serve as a tool to impact the world in area that is relevant to their own interests.

This is perhaps one of the greatest opportunities we have today: helping learners discover a reason and purpose for learning.

Passion, Curiosity, Imagination, Critical Thinking, and Grit

Peter Diamandis often gets asked a question about raising children in times of exponential change. "So, Peter, what will you teach your kids given this explosion of exponential technologies?"

"In the near term (this next decade) the lingua franca is coding and machine learning. Any kid graduating college with these skills today can get a job. But this too, will be disrupted in the near future by AI. Long-term, it is passion, curiosity, imagination, critical thinking, and grit."

Passion

"You'd be amazed at how many people don't have a mission in life. A calling, something to jolt them out of bed every morning," writes Diamandis.

Developing a passion is a key. It can be understood as the driving force, the true motivation behind work or any other endeavor.

"The best moments in our lives are not the passive, receptive, relaxing times," says Mihaly Csikszentmihalyi, author of *Flow,* "the best moments usually occur if a person's body or mind is stretched to its limits in a voluntary effort to accomplish something difficult and worthwhile."

In this state of flow, a student-worker-preneur can be completely absorbed in an activity, especially one involving creativity. During this "optimal experience" you feel strong, alert, in effortless control, unselfconscious, and at the peak of your abilities, according to the author. The key to this is setting challenges that are neither too demanding nor too simple for a person's abilities.

In a talk at Singularity University, Ray Kurzweil, Google Director of Engineering, was asked "When robots are everywhere, what will humans be good for?" His answer was that, if under the logic that automation will take away a big chunk of the drudgery, the work humans don't enjoy doing, it will leave us with more time to explore what we want to explore. Part of his advice then was to "develop a passion."

American astrophysicist, cosmologist, author, and science communicator Neil deGrasse Tyson says that "what you need, above all else, is a love for your subject, whatever it is. You've got to be so deeply in love with your subject that when curve balls are thrown, when hurdles are put in place, you've got the energy to overcome them."

Developing a passion is closely linked with other three ingredients: curiosity, imagination, and critical thinking.

Curiosity

Jeff Bezos said this about success and innovation: "If you want to invent, if you want to do any innovation, anything new, you're going to have failures because you need to experiment. I think the amount of useful invention you do is directly proportional to the number of experiments you can run per week per month per year."

At an award's acceptance speech in London, Google co-founder Larry Page, said "we tried a lot of things, most of which failed." He elaborated that when they set out to create the world's biggest search engine, they were just pursuing their interests, hopefully arriving at something that would be useful. The key takeaway comes in the form of direct advice from Page: "You should pick areas that you think are interesting, that could be valuable, or where there's a lot of activity. I was interested at links because I knew no one else was interested in them, and I figured you could probably do something with them." We can infer from this that curiosity is key to arriving at what actually interests you.

The author of *Silicon Guild*, Peter Sims, points out the work of INSEAD business school professors who surveyed over 3,000 executives and interviewed 500 people who had either started innovative companies or invented new products. They concluded that a number of the innovative entrepreneurs learned to follow their curiosity. Without curiosity it would be impossible to expand the frontiers of what is possible.

Videogame inventor Will Wright, co-founder of Maxis (which became part of Electronic Arts) points out the importance of the joy of discovery: "It's all about learning on your terms, rather than a teacher explaining stuff to you." SimCity, one of Wright's creations, is an example of this.

Curiosity and the joy of discovery are closely linked to imagination, another quality identified by Diamandis.

Imagination

"Entrepreneurs and visionaries imagine the world (and the future) they want to live in, and then they create it. Kids happen to be some of the most imaginative humans around... it is critical that they know how important and liberating imagination can be," says Diamandis.

"Imagination is one of humanity's greatest qualities," says Richard Branson, founder of Virgin, "without it, there would be no innovation, advancement or technology, and the world would be a very dull place."

Critical thinking

"Critical thinking is probably the hardest lesson to teach kids. It takes time and experience, and you have to reinforce habits like investigation, curiosity, skepticism, and so on", says Diamandis.

A movement called Philosophy for Children, also known as P4C and under the auspices of Stanford University, began with the late philosopher Matthew Lipman's 1969 novel Harry Stottlemeier's *Discovery*. The novel and accompanying teacher manual were designed to help children in K-12 learn how to think for themselves.

Dr. Peter Facione, who spearheaded the American Philosophical Association's international study to define critical thinking elaborates on the meaning and importance of critical thinking: "We understand critical thinking to be purposeful, self-regulatory judgment which results in interpretation, analysis, evaluation, and inference, as well as explanation of the evidential, conceptual, methodological, criteriological, or contextual considerations upon which that judgment is based.... The ideal critical thinking is habitually inquisitive, well-informed, trustful of reason, open-minded, flexible, fair-minded in evaluation, honest in facing personal biases, prudent in making judgments, willing to reconsider, clear about issues, orderly in complex matters, diligent in seeking relevant information, reasonable in the selection of criteria, focused in inquiry, and persistent in seeking results which are the subject and the circumstances of inquiry".

Ad Astra school: "to the stars"

Speaking of education for disruptors, it makes sense to examine how disruptors are teaching their own kids. Elon Musk's disruptive endeavors span finance (PayPal), solar energy (Solar City), cars (Tesla), space exploration (SpaceX) and now, education. He didn't like his kids' school, so he started his own. It is called Ad Astra which means "to the stars". For now the school is also serving kids of SpaceX employees. One of its features is a focus on problem solving. "Let's say you're trying to teach people about how engines work," said Musk to a media outlet. "A more traditional approach would be saying 'We're going to teach all about screwdrivers and wrenches'. This is a very difficult way to do it. A much better way would be, like, 'Here's the engine. Now let's take it apart. How are we going to take it apart? Oh, you need a screwdriver'." This is clear approach to ignite motivation and critical thinking. "It makes more sense to cater the education to match their aptitude and abilities," also remarked Musk. Interestingly, Musk reports that his kids "really love going to school" so much that "they actually think vacations are too long; they want to go back to school."

The Montessori approach

In a Wall Street Journal article, Peter Sims points out that "the Montessori educational approach might be the surest route to joining the creative elite." He cites that it is so overrepresented by the school's alumni that one might suspect a Montessori Mafia. Graduates include Google's founders Larry Page and Sergey Brin, Amazon's Jeff Bezos, and Wikipedia founder Jimmy Wales.

In an interview with Barbara Walters, Larry Page said: "we both went to Montessori school, and I think it was part of that training, of not following rules and orders and being self-motivated, questioning what's going on in the world, doing things a little bit differently."

The Montessori learning method was founded by Maria Montessori and it features a collaborative environment without grades or tests, multi-aged classrooms, as well as self-directed learning and discovery for long blocks of time, primarily for young children between the ages of two and a half and seven.

The approach nurtures creativity, taking after the work of inventors who typically improvise, experiment, fail, and retest. Sims points out that inventors such as Henry Ford and Thomas Edison were voracious inquisitive learners.

In a world flooded with often-conflicting ideas, baseless claims, misleading headlines, negative news and misinformation, you have to think critically to find the signal in the noise, explains Diamandis.

Grit

Finally, grit is seen as "passion and perseverance in pursuit of long-term goals," and it has recently been widely acknowledged as one of the most important predictors of and contributors to success.

Pinterest was launched in 2010. The story of co-founder Ben Silbermann is a great testament of perseverance. In 2008, Silbermann decided to quit a job he hated. However, he didn't know what he wanted to build, so built an app called Tote... and it flopped. He then decided to try a new idea, a site for collecting things, and it was rejected by many investors. He made fifty different versions of the site, launched it and got 200 initial users. Silbermann personally wrote welcome emails to his first 7,000 users, and in this process he discovered that his early adopters were "moms". The rest, as they say, is history. Today Pinterest is home to over 500 employees. The company recently doubled its valuation to over $11 billion.

Education and life as process of self-directed learning

Sergey Brin said "there are many important things to life aside from financial or career success, and in fact, it's not necessarily the ultimate success that motivates you, it's the process of getting there; the technology, the products that you build. I am not too concerned about finding something to do, though I do think it will be based on doing things that I really enjoy, and not have some end goal in mind."

Being exposed to new people and ideas

Speaking of predictors of career success, according to Ron Burt, one of the world's top network scientists, being in an open network instead of a closed one is the best predictor of career success, a discovery based on multiple, peer-reviewed studies.

Burt explained that if you are a member of a "large, open network where you are the link between people from different clusters", as opposed to being a member of a "small, closed network where you are connected to people who already know each other" you have a much higher chance of overall career success

"The more you repeatedly hear the same ideas, which reaffirm what you already believe. The further you go toward an open network, the more you're exposed to new ideas." Simmons concludes, based on network science, that people who are members of open networks, and hence open to all sorts of new information, are significantly more successful than members of small, closed networks.

The relevance of Science, Technology, Engineering, Math (STEM) education

The other key distinction in terms of education directly correlates with the first part of the book: emerging technologies.

The fact that a number of highly disruptive technologies are coming of age in a relatively short time frame presents an opportunity for student-worker-preneurs focused on Science, Technology, Engineering, Math (STEM). This is due to the competitive advantage that comes from being the first movers in those particular technologies.

Software guru, Jesse Stay, comments that, "there will be a much stronger, and greater need for engineering, and STEM-related jobs."

Overall employment trends by the US Labor Market Statistics, point out that graduates of Science, Technology, Engineering, and Mathematics (STEM) majors are and will be the most demanded areas. In the United States, STEM employment grew three times more than non-STEM employment over the last twelve years, and is expected to grow twice as fast by 2018.

Emerging technology companies will demand specialists in the areas we have reviewed, including 3D printing, advanced robotics, big data, biotech, nanotech, etc. presenting an economic opportunity of close to $20 trillion in the next 10 years. This will require specialized graduates in a wide array of industries, according to McKinsey & Co. However, as reported by Manpower and various studies, even at present, tech companies are struggling to find qualified candidates, resulting in unfilled positions and reduced growth.

Importance of the Soft skills: the 4 C's

Perhaps some of the hardest skills to teach, the so called soft skills, may be the most important ones in a new economy. While we have already referenced creativity and critical thinking, communication and collaboration will also be essential enablers for the modern student-worker-preneur. Referred to by some educators as the 4 C's, these soft skills are already instrumental in the workplace.

Leaders and Entrepreneurs

At the intersection of the technical and interpersonal competencies we can appreciate that two traits emerge: leadership and entrepreneurship. Arguably this is the intended result of the educational system. Moreover, I conclude that a focus on developing leaders and entrepreneurs might be the right educational aim, as this in consonance with the workplace shifts occurring over the next two decades, where less repetitive and predictable tasks are performed and where higher order tasks, in terms of cognitive complexity, will be the norm.

One of the projects we have started at Emtechub is precisely to identify young talented individuals from around the world who are doing impressive work with emerging technologies. They are emerging as leaders in their fields, addressing real world problems. We call it the Emerging Technology Leaders Global Initiative. Emtechleaders (for short) is a non-profit initiative that will help inspire young students around the world to pursue STEM careers, with a focus on emerging technologies.

Inspiring the young and young at heart

Neil deGrasse Tyson affirms that "Once you have an innovation culture, even those who are not scientists or engineers, poets, actors, journalists, they, as communities, embrace the meaning of what it is to be scientifically literate. They embrace the concept of an innovation culture. They vote in ways that promote it. They don't fight science and they don't fight technology."

Putting it all together

The Berkeley Alumni magazine points out that the inventor of the CRISP-cas9 DNA editing method, Jennifer Doudna "came to UC Berkeley from Yale in 2002 with a reputation for working side-by-side with Nobel laureates and having a knack for building alliances with other creative thinkers. She was also known for her brilliance at teasing out the purpose of biomolecules and for an uncanny ability to glean the shapes of the virtually invisible: the remarkable molecular machinery that spins within living cells". ·

This is a very telling statement. It not only reveals the importance of the hard technical skills, but how important it is to be able to collaborate, and to think creatively.

It strengthens the idea that the way forward in education has to do with a mix of hard and soft skills.

High tech companies are not only looking for proficiency in the hard, technical side of technology, but on the soft skills. In a Forbes article, Rich Milgram, CEO of career network <u>Beyond</u>, is quoted saying, "And more about how you think systems through and work within the context of the team. Learning a technology is the easy part. Having the mindset to apply it, having the mindset and logic to process it, being thorough and detail-oriented while doing so, these are the critical skills."

Teaching with automation in mind

If we accept that machines will progressively take over predictable and repetitive labor, it makes more sense to teach with a focus on the tasks that *cannot* be performed by AI systems. This will become more evident as automation advances in the coming years. Hence, it makes more sense to focus on nurturing a skillset of both hard and soft abilities aimed at solving complex problems, out of the reach of automated systems, at least for now.

2

The future of upstream oil and gas from a well integrity perspective

FEDERICO JUAREZ, ENG.*

Well Integrity Engineer based in Norway.

Oil and gas (O&G) are found and brought safely to surface by drilling and completing wells. A well is a borehole which is drilled in order to discover or delimit a petroleum deposit and/or to produce petroleum or water for injection purposes, to inject gas, water or other medium, or monitor well parameters (Norwegian Petroleum Directorate, well definitions, 2015). There are several categories of wells mainly, exploration and development wells.

To design, drill and complete a well, the work and collaboration of many disciplines is necessary. The following diagram shows the different disciplines, company areas (or departments) and approaches involved in the design and construction process of a development well.

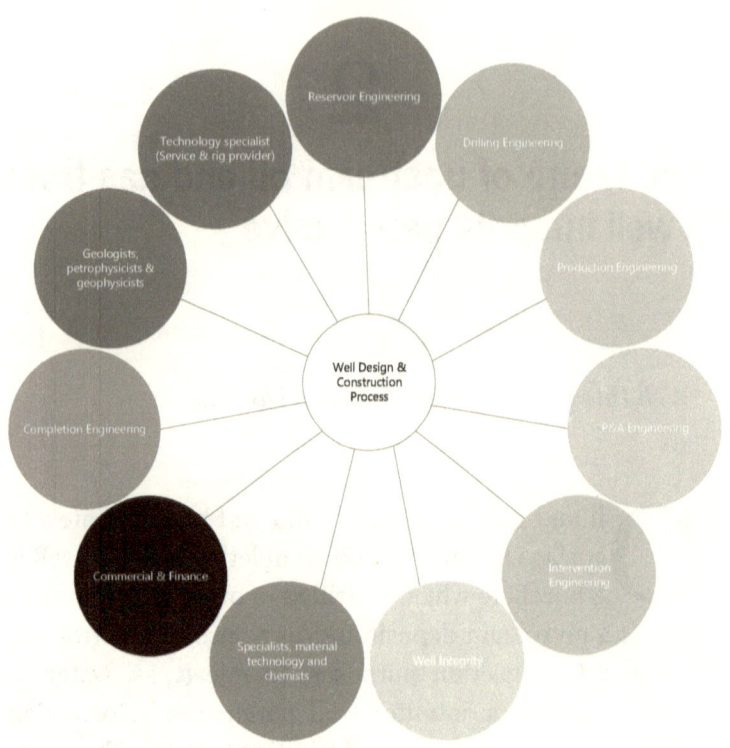

Figure 1: Petroleum disciplines and company areas involved in the well design and construction process.

However, drilling and completing a well is just a *baby step* in the well's lifecycle. The lifetime of a well varies depending on its location (e.g. onshore, offshore, and subsea), purpose (e.g. injection, production, exploration, appraisal, wildcat, storage, observation), reservoir properties and content, technology used, etc. Interestingly, most of a well's lifetime is related to production/injection operations whereas a very short period is connected to construction, repair and abandonment.

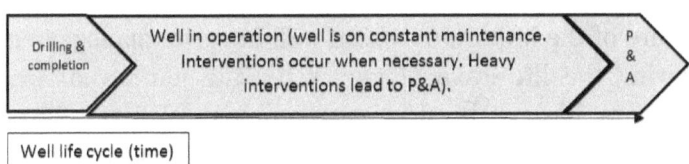

| Drilling & completion | Well in operation (well is on constant maintenance. Interventions occur when necessary. Heavy interventions lead to P&A). | P & A |

Well life cycle (time)

The different petroleum disciplines participate in the well construction process but they are not held responsible for monitoring the *health* of the well. Well integrity (WI) is the multidisciplinary approach that monitors the well's *health*. It additionally ensures that all wells are drilled, completed, produced, maintained, repaired, plugged, and abandoned safely, with all the necessary well barrier elements in place and in compliance with local government regulations.

There are different definitions on what well integrity is. Currently, the official definition is taken from the Norwegian well integrity standard, NORSOK D-010: *"the application of technical and organizational solutions during the well life cycle to reduce the risk for an uncontrolled incident to happen."* The well life cycle spans the time when the borehole is initially drilled up until the time the well is completely plugged and abandoned.

Well integrity is an essential aspect of the well design, construction, and operational process. It allows operators to better manage and design wells to transport hydrocarbons safely to the surface avoiding, uncontrolled release of fluids to the atmosphere and to the surroundings.

Well integrity is a fairly new field within petroleum engineering. Incidents related to uncontrolled release of hydrocarbons and loss of containment (e.g. Macondo, Ixtoc I, Elgin, etc.) have made the O&G industry more aware of the important role of well integrity management during the life cycle of any well. The journey of well integrity has not been an easy one and WI has evolved from database management into almost a new discipline (Hopmans Paul, 2013). With more than 50% of field investments going to drilling and well activities (Norwegian Petroleum Directorate, Recovery from producing fields, 2014), well integrity is fundamental to assess the risk of operations, compliance to requirements and identify failures so that best practices can be improved and/or created to improve the well designs and optimize hydrocarbon recovery.

Although well integrity focuses mainly on development wells, it also assesses the risk for loss of integrity on exploration and relief wells. The challenges will vary depending on the well location and its purpose.

We have previously defined the different types of wells, however, the following table describes those concepts more in detail including some examples of the common well integrity challenges depending on the type of well.

Table 1: description of the different types of wells, drill uses, and well integrity related challenges.

Type of well	Use	Example of well integrity challenge
Exploration	Well drilled in order to establish the existence of a possible petroleum deposit or to acquire information in order to delimit and establish a deposit.	Well isolation barriers (e.g. cement plugs and cement outside casings), well monitoring after abandonment, communication with development wellbores

	Wildcat and appraisal wells are a form of exploration wells with different exploratory functions.	in the area or storage wells (i.e. CO_2 storage wellbore nearby)
Relief	Well drilled to recover control over a lost wellbore most likely due to a major well integrity incident (i.e. blowout)	Formation integrity, cement channeling, valve failures (BOP failures), uncontrolled communication between wellbores
Development	Well drilled to recover hydrocarbons out from the subsurface. Development wells can be production, injection and observation wells or, a combination thereof. Storage wells are also classified as development wells	Lack of isolation barriers, leakage through downhole well equipment, sustained casing pressure, communication between wellbores (e.g. injector-producer through overburden), formation subsidence, wellhead fatigue, corrosion, production chemistry problems (scale, wax, paraffin),

The examples mentioned in the table above illustrate the common equipment or components failures that can eventually lead to a system failure and loss of well integrity (e.g. blowouts). In well integrity management, component failure and system failure are referred to as well barrier failure and well integrity failure respectively.

Well barrier failure is regularly used to refer to the failure of individual or multiple well barriers (e.g. production tubing, cement behind casing, downhole safety valve, etc.) whereas a well integrity failure can be defined as a sequential failure of all well barriers in a leakage path leading to a well integrity incident. well integrity failure is then a consequence of consecutive well barrier failures. Distinction between these two concepts is also done by (King and King, 2013) and (Davies R.J. et al., 2014). Finally, a well integrity incident is the result of a well integrity failure leading to a loss of containment. It can be defined as an event in which an uncontrolled release of underground fluids to the surface, personnel or surroundings occur.

The main objective of well integrity is to prevent well integrity incidents from happening; hence, it is important to distinguish between well barrier failure, well integrity failure and well integrity incident.

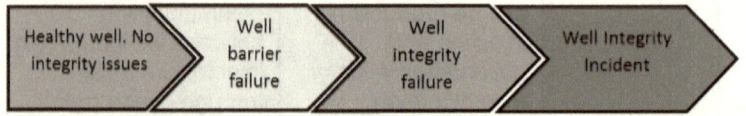

Figure 2: Evolution from the well integrity status of a well into a well integrity incident. The colors do not reflect well integrity status or compliance to regulations. Colors in the diagram above are used as reference code being, red completely unacceptable condition, loss of integrity and containment, and green the optimum state of any well.

The following bowtie diagram shows a relationship example between well barrier failure and well integrity incident.

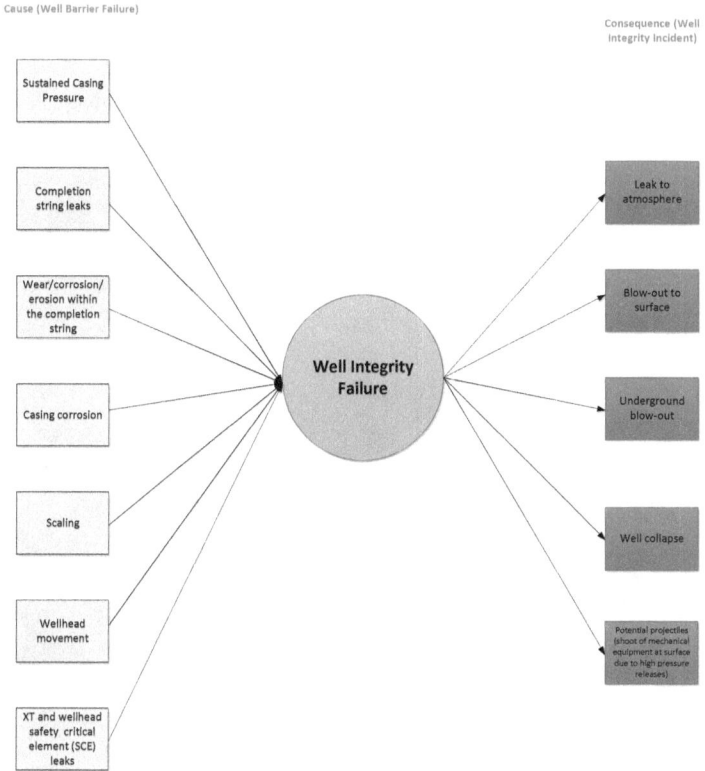

The challenge for well integrity is to adequately manage well barrier elements, identify source of failures, organize well information and structure decision making. Therefore, oil and gas operators should create well integrity management systems to steer well integrity more efficiently.

Today, well integrity uses a KPI system to categorize and differentiate regulatory barrier integrity status of oil and gas wells. The categorization system used was created by the Norwegian oil and gas association (Norwegian oil and gas Association, 2011) and is based in the traffic light principle and in the two well barrier philosophy. It is a

KPI system currently adopted worldwide and accepted by several regulatory agencies.

Table 2: well integrity KPI category system taken from NoG guideline 117: Recommended guidelines for well integrity

Category	Green	Yellow	Orange	Red
Descrip -tion	Healthy well-no or minor issue	One barrier degraded, the other is intact	One barrier failure and the other is intact or a single failure may lead to leak to surface.	One barrier failure and the other is degraded/ not verified, or leak to surface.
Associa -ted risk	Comparable to that of an identical new well.	Incremental risk which is not negligible compared to that of an identical new well with design in compliance with all regulations	Higher than the risk associated with an identical new well with design in compliance with all regulations.	Considerable higher than the risk associated with an identical new well with design in compliance with all regulations.
Compli- ance with regula- tions	Within regulations	Within regulations	Typically outside regulations	Typically outside regulations

Typical actions	No immediate repairs or mitigating measures	No immediate repairs or mitigating measures but usually mitigating measures will be planned.	Repairs and/or mitigations to put the well in normal operation but usually no urgent or immediate need for action	Repairs and/or mitigations to put the well in normal operation and there will usually be an immediate and urgent need for action.

This system currently allows both operators and government regulatory agencies to have a better overview of the integrity status of the wells and to distinguish from the wells and fields that are compliant to local requirements (i.e. green and yellow category) from those that are not (i.e. orange and red). However, to be compliant to requirements does not necessarily mean a well or field represents a high or low risk for a well integrity incident to happen.

For example, in Norway in 2014, 14 operator companies in the Norwegian Continental Shelf reported a total of 1918 active wells (exploration and P&A wellbores were not included). Seven point six percent were wells not compliant to local regulations while 92.4 per cent were compliant (The Petroleum Safety Authority of Norway, 2014). But, from the wells that were reported incompliant to Norwegian regulations which one is the most critical of all and why? If an intervention or workover campaign was to start which well shall the operator in the NCS prioritize and why?

The Norwegian example is a good reference to address such interrogatives. Nevertheless, the number of wells in Norway is small compared to the rest of the world. Davies et al. (2014) found out that there are more than four million onshore Oil and gas wells and more than 25 000 offshore Oil and gas wells that have been drilled and completed globally. Subsea wells make a small portion of the total number of offshore wells (currently estimated 2500-3000 subsea wells in the world). How can a single operator (i.e. IOC) apply the same well integrity KPI system if government regulations and requirements vary between countries and/or regions?

One of the main challenges for well integrity Management today is to distinguish between being compliant to local regulations and the risk associated for well integrity incidents to happen in a well with and without well barrier failures.

The presence of at least two well barrier envelopes, comprised of multiple barrier elements provides layers of protection against unexpected and unwanted release of fluids to the surface and environment. However, the existence of well barriers does not entirely eliminate the potential for well integrity incidents to occur. Depending on factors such as well design, reservoir pressure (flow potential), the properties of the fluids, and the reliability of the well barrier elements, the overall risk posed to the personnel, environment and surroundings can vary.

Today, risk assessments in well integrity begin to be utilized to provide with means for decision making in situations and cases where information is limited and where the KPI system falls short. Nonetheless, to assess risk, it is necessary to understand what risk is. Until recently, the most common accepted definition of risk was the product between the probability for an event to happen and the consequences such event would bring with it. Now, new perspectives on risk have been developed and it is becoming increasingly accepted to replace probability with uncertainty in the definition in addition to include extra variables accounting for the degree of knowledge available at the time of the assessment.

Recent developments in well integrity industry standards encourage the use of risk assessment techniques for integrity evaluation and criticality assessments in a proactive, reactive and interactive way. Nowadays, the oil and gas industry use numerical risk acceptance criteria. But as Aven & Krohn (2013) suggest, these are often probability-based cut-off criteria and as risk is more than just probability it becomes at times hard to justify and quantify that risk is acceptable if the computes probability value is below a specific value and not acceptable otherwise.

Thus, due to the nature of the challenges well integrity face and the magnitude of the unexplored scientific field ahead, well integrity will most likely evolve into a new discipline within Petroleum Sciences and Engineering.

In ten years from now, well integrity will most likely turn from a multidisciplinary approach into a new risk based engineering discipline. It will continue to safeguard the law and the regulations but as well integrity will develop a new understanding of risk and risk assessment tools, it will also be able to challenge the basis of the laws and regulations currently governing the Oil and gas upstream industry.

Moreover, for well integrity to be efficient, structured and proactive, it will need to be independent from Drilling, Completion, Intervention and P&A activities in the management chain. Another possibility is for well integrity to take over Drilling and Well operations to ensure these activities are performed in compliance to local government regulations and within HSE acceptable risk levels at all times.

Another great challenge for well integrity in the future will be to assess and monitor the integrity of permanently plugged & abandoned wells. It is likely that in the future many wells in the world will become permanently P&A. It will be imperative that proper monitoring and follow up processes are in place particularly, after the well abandonment, so that risk associated with both future drilling and human activities (e.g. agriculture, fishing, and farming) is minimized. The P&A design for current O&G wells should be based on the eternal perspective. In the long term, the challenge will be how to ensure eternal integrity of well barrier envelopes and elements in the wells that have been permanently P&A. How to ensure that the more than four million O&G wells worldwide will never leak either in the upcoming decade or in thousands years from now. Who will be held responsible if a permanently plugged and abandoned offshore field leaks to ocean surface in 500 years from now? What if an earthquake provokes a loss of containment of a permanently plugged and abandoned onshore gas field with high content of H$_2$S near a developed urban area in 200 years from now? Who shall repair the wells and replace the plugs? Why were not well barriers designed accordingly to ensure well integrity from eternal perspective? These are some questions and scenarios that well integrity will deal with in the upcoming future. In the next 10 years, well integrity should answer or at least help to find the answer to the following questions:

How to categorize the integrity and risk status of permanently plugged and abandoned wells from an eternal perspective?

How to permanently monitor P&A wells?

The legal terms and regulations to establish control over permanently plugged and abandoned wellbores. Who shall be responsible? What happens if the operator company disappears in 50 years' time and some of the wells leak to surface in 100 years' time?

There are many challenges ahead for well integrity. The journey of well integrity will continue to be exponential, analytical and innovative.

To achieve the goals, well integrity will need to redefine the concept of risk, combine risk assessments (both qualitative and quantitative) together with standards and government regulations to allow operator companies and regulatory government agencies to challenge and stimulate technology innovation that will improve the management of both producing and abandoned Oil and gas fields and ensure well integrity and subsurface containment eternally.

Ultimately, the destiny of well integrity is to merge with Surface Containment Assurance to ensure that hydrocarbons and underground fluids are contained under the Earth's surface forever.

References

Davies R.J. et al. (2014). Oil and gas wells and their integrity: Implications for shale and unconventional resource exploitation. Marine and Petroleum Geology. ELSEVIER.

Hopmans Paul. (2013). Journey of well integrity. SPE Web Event - Joureny of well integrity. Web: SPE.

King and King. (2013). SPE 166142: Environmental Risk Arising From Well-Construction Failure - Differences between barrier and well failure and estimates of failure frequency across common well types, locations and well age. SPE.

Norwegian oil and gas Association (NoG). (2011, June 06). 117 - Recommended Guidelines for well integrity. Retrieved July 27, 2015, from https://www.norskoljeoggass.no/no/Publikasjoner/Retningslinjer/Boring/117-Recommended-guidelines-for-Well-Integrity/

Norwegian Petroleum Directorate. (2014). Recovery from producing fields. In NPD, Petroleum resources on the Norwegian Continental Shelf. NPD.

Norwegian Petroleum Directorate. (2015, 10 18). Well definitions. Retrieved from Oljedirektoratet - Well definitions: http://www.npd.no/en/Topics/Wells/Temaartikler/Well-definitions/

The Petroleum Safety Authority of Norway. (2014). RNNP sammendragsrapport. Retrieved August 7, 2015, from http://www.ptil.no/getfile.php/PDF/RNNP%202014/RNNP2014_sammendrag.pdf

3
Linking personal goals and competences to create innovation and regional development
JESUS ESCANDON, ENG.*

Co-founder of Tyeca, President of the Swedish Chapter of Red Global MX, and Coordinator of Entrepreneurship and Innovation at Red Global MX Europe.

When I was a small boy, I used to dream that one day I would become a technology expert and entrepreneur. My goal to accomplish is to improve people's daily life with technology. Technology must be personal and useful. Technology is not a tool, it is an instrument, and therefore it is not intuitive and needs to be taught.

I would like to share my personal story and hopefully by going through my experience I can show you why I believe that our future centers on people's personal development.

For me, a personal story is linked to personal relationships where goals and competences are the key factors to establish relationships. In my story, I have connected with and collaborated with a variety of fantastic individuals. Having fun is the key ingredient making our stories a great odyssey.

The establishment of Tyeca Technologies AB

The story of Tyeca Technology Limited dates back to 1998 when two Mexican students happened to meet each other in Mexico City. They became good friends and started doing different projects together.

Hector was born in Mexico City. He now lives in Sweden as a Swedish citizen with his family. Back in 2005 he came to Sweden to study a Master's program in Computer Science at the School of Engineering at Jönköping University.

With two friends who were also studying in Mexico City at Tec de Monterrey they decided to apply to Jönköping University to a graduate program. After being accepted they all came to Sweden to pursue their degree. Since then Hector has lived in Jönköping.

Hector studied Engineering in Computer Science and graduated in Mexico before coming to Sweden and being part of the Master Program. When he was in Mexico, Hector was deeply involved in his family business. Almost fifteen years ago, Hector's father founded a company which offers business consultancy and management services. The first task for Hector when he started working in his family business was related to fixing computers. As time passed he started getting more knowledgeable about software development. Later on, he eventually became responsible for server operations, computer systems, software development, and for software architectures.

Hector and I have remained friends since college. As undergraduate students we created our first business project, exploiting the opportunity of having unused old computers from our families business. Spotting the need at that time for people to access internet, we ran an Internet cafe for some time. We discovered that Internet access was a secondary need, people visited the cafe because we helped them and taught them how to use technology. This was at the time where the concept of a personal email was still something new for most of the population in Mexico. After that we also worked with each other in a couple of family-related business projects.

Then Hector and I decided to work together to create our own software consultancy, providing services to our family business to integrate bespoke software solutions, in addition to their existing consultancy services. This was still as undergraduate students, about 9 months before Hector moved to Sweden, when we still did not know that our personal and business plans would involve moving to Sweden.

When Hector completed the move, first he started working as a sole trader, continuing to develop software for our end customers through the consultancy family business in Mexico. We worked long distance for the first two years while Hector was in Sweden and I, in Mexico.

I, Jesus Escandón, was born in Mexico City. I came to Sweden in 2008, to pursue a computer science Master's program at the University of Jönköping. I met Hector when we were studying at the Tec de Monterrey, the University in Mexico City. Since coming to Sweden I have lived in Jönköping City with my family.

Through my childhood I was, and still am, deeply surrounded by an academic environment as both of my parents work in education. I got my first computer at the age of six and since then I started my interest in computers and technology. I was always around computers, following my parents to research centers. A good portion of my play time included seeing what they were doing for work.

I graduated as a Computer Science Engineer in Mexico. Since I was student, I have worked in my family business. My mother used to own and run a private junior high school while she was also working for the educational sector in the Mexican Government. She ran a company in the education sector managing different projects with regional and national impact in Mexico. I grew up along my family business. When I was a teenager, I delivered classes to students in the family school. Later I started to take care of the computer lab at the school. I was given more responsibilities as I matured, to prepare for taking over control of the business at some stage. Now I'm leading the team that is controlling the technology division of the family business.

I also worked with Hector in projects in relation to his family business and before that we ran an Internet café while being undergraduate students at the university in Mexico. When Hector move to Sweden and I was still in Mexico we continued working together, as about 9 months before Hector move to Sweden we have decided that we want to create our technology consultancy company a personal goal of creating our own business that each one of us had and the only way we want to succeed was working together as friends.

In 2011 in Sweden, along with another friend we founded Tyeca Technologies AB, a consultancy company developing software with its target market in both Mexico and Sweden.

The development: startup stage, growing stage and transforming stage 2005-2015

In our individual background the development process of our business concept of Tyeca Technologies AB started even long before the company was established as a limited company. This process started in 2005 when Hector first came to Sweden.

Hector started his computer science Master's program in August 2005. During this time, Hector was still working on different software development projects remotely from Sweden together with me in Mexico for his family business. His role was to take care of developing software needed for these projects in Mexico, and the fact that Hector was in Sweden was a plus to our customers who liked the idea of their software being developed taking in consideration the new knowledge and perspective of a society like the Swedish.

During the time Hector was studying, two years to be precise, he did not have a long term plan in Sweden. His plan was to keep working remotely from Sweden. Our third partner, at that time, was also working locally with Hector and remotely with Mexico. I was in Mexico working for our final customer, traveling inside Mexico City and other states in Mexico, at the customer's various locations. We were developing these projects for Hector's family company. When we were about 23 or 24 years old we had to solve on how to work with a seven hour time zone difference. We were simultaneously developing software in two continents with limited options for communicating. I was traveling around Mexico working on local office hours, with team meetings scheduled for either 1:00 a.m. Mexico City time or 1:00 a.m. in Stockholm.

In 2007, we needed to find a way to formalize our operations, so Hector decided to register himself as a sole trader in Sweden. This was a decisive moment for us to see Sweden as a long term establishment.

In 2008 I arrived to Sweden and integrated to our development team in Jönköping. We kept on working in the same manner: receiving software development projects from Mexico through our families' companies, getting the work done in Sweden and sending invoices from Sweden to Mexico.

There wasn't a specific date, but at some point, as a result of individual decisions, we decided to stay in Sweden and establish ourselves here.

In 2011, we got a project from a Swedish company. As part of the requirements, as we learned, the company needed to work with a limited company rather than with sole traders; we decided it was time to incorporate Tyeca Technologies Limited Company in 2011. Before this we were already shifting our focus a little more to the Swedish market. Now the plan of residing in Sweden temporarily for postgrad education had evolved to a long term plan.

At this time we felt quite settled in Sweden so we started considering of how to promote our business in software development and get customers in Sweden. We thought about ways to make potential customers known that there were these Mexican engineers located in Science Park, Jönköping, who were successfully developing software for big Mexican companies. This was a complex endeavor indeed, a steep learning curve which was completely out of our comfort zone and competences, not to mention that we had zero contacts or local references.

We were determined to succeed so we took into account what our imagination, friends and mentors suggested. Throughout the process we were in a constant mode of spotting opportunities, because—and I know how this may sound—failure was not an option. Just like that another business concept was created. Our office is located in Science Park of Jönköping and staff members' companies located in the same office building reached the founders of Tyeca asking for help fixing computers and hardware, configuring local networks and peripheral devices. This led to the idea of creating a service of computer repair serving the needs of private customers and business. We thought that when we solve a problem using Geeklab computer repair service for a private customer with their technology, these customers can help Tyeca approach and look for potential customers with the companies that they work for.

At this time we had a project with our first corporate customer in Sweden so we concentrated ourselves on that project and had a temporary break from the IT computer repair service.

In 2012 we started working again with our computer repair service, Geeklab. We started to really explore what we had found. We realized that Geeklab had much more potential as a way to open windows of opportunity for Tyeca. We put more resources in developing the service. We worked on creating the concept for private consumers and businesses. At the beginning, it was not clear for us what to offer and how to proceed when receiving a service order. We were clear in our belief and purpose of helping people think about the application of our knowledge and experience within technology, this is why we do it, and it is what drives all our past, current and future efforts.

During the development process at this stage in Geeklab, we faced several problems in order to make the service friendlier to customers approaching Geeklab. Customers felt that staff members were so technically advanced that they were afraid to approach the company. We realized that Geeklab had too technical of an image getting in the way, something understandable for a bunch of engineers.

In 2013 with such feedback, we started working on creating a less technical image. Instead of having an image of some parts of an electronic device, Geeklab was portrayed as a cartoon character, a geek being ready going around to fix computers when customers call. This was the start of a creation process of what is known today as Geeklab.

From there we continued to develop the concept of Geeklab into a separate brand of Tyeca Technologies. Geeklab focuses on the Swedish market targeting on private customers and businesses. Tyeca Technologies still focus in Mexico, but now with stronger influences of the Swedish context; we had created new business alliances to develop and promote opportunities in Mexico and Sweden.

What has Tyeca done to link personal goals and competences to facilitate innovation and regional development?

From the point of view of Tyeca, the answer might be by now almost like a conclusion: there were two individuals who became friends in college. They had a dream that pushed them into creating a Swedish company that works for Mexican companies and local business, providing local and international services with a global perspective. We actively facilitate new business opportunities for our business network which I prefer to call business friends, and these opportunities go beyond our business, as we help Mexican business and Swedish business. But this conclusion is almost intuitive. There is still a question about Geeklab that you might also have in mind.

How does a computing engineer turn into a talented graphic designer with communication and marketing skills?

The answer might strike you: *You just simply can't.*

In Tyeca we have been extreme fortunate to have found a place we call home, with people who have become our family. In this fantastic adventure many have helped us and supported us in the fulfillment of our dreams.

This is also related to our fundamental value in Tyeca of being helpful. When we face the challenge of building a brand we knew that we had to find talented individuals who believed in what we were trying to accomplish. Looking to hire a local Swedish marketing agency was out of the question due to our budget constraints.

Our actions of being actively helpful gave us the answer. In that moment when we were looking on how to solve our challenge, we were approached by a student from the Monterrey (Mexico) Campus of the Tec de Monterrey University, who happened to be doing an exchange semester at Jönköping University. We had previously conducted outreach amongst new international students from Mexico, giving them our contact details the moment they set foot on campus at Jönköping University. We strived to help them with the process of adaptation and with the many questions that arise when you just arrive as an exchange student. The student was looking for us to help him, he wanted to have a professional practice in our company as he was looking to have an international practice that would count in his academic records. From our perspective we needed a talented and engaged person with the competences we were lacking. This was a clear win-win model. We tried it and the results were just amazing.

With this experience and knowledge, we developed a model: linking individuals, with the focus on linking personal goals with the company's vision. Then we identified what competences needed to be learned, including the cultural and social skills. Once we have this link, the intern and the company team execute our Program of Innovation and Development. This Program has been designed based in our way of doing projects in Tyeca and the entrepreneurship experience and knowledge. Once the team finishes the program we have a successfully executed project for the company, a team in the company that has learned and practiced those lessons in multicultural competences, entrepreneurship, leadership and management, planning and *soft power*. An intern with a professional and international experience, that has created personal links and international networks.

The model has been working since August 2013 and each new semester more exchange students approached us, as the students that previously been practicing with us when they go back they recommend to more students that will make an exchange semester in Jönköping to contact us and now we have contact with them even before they arrive at Jönköping University. We are now looking to establish a formal program with the Tec de Monterrey University system in Mexico.

A common feedback is that after a student finishes our practice program, they expressed that, in comparison to their fellow students, they were going beyond just taking courses, they had an experience that was really an international and multicultural exchange.

Conclusion

Fostering understanding among business cultures and highlighting the potential benefits of Small Medium Enterprises (SMEs) is both the present and the future of local business. Entrepreneurs can and should be encouraged to venture outside their own countries, as individuals who have been exposed to new tasks, industries, cultures, and abilities, become assets beyond their area of discipline or expertise.

International business projects, driven by individuals with distinctive and complementary skills should be supported to foster increasing international trade development.

In this context, the story of the individual, his or her experience, becomes increasingly relevant. The *who are you, who are you becoming*, and *what do you want* are questions that will continue to define the type of engagement that you are capable and willing to do. This conditions skill and ability to personal goals and vision, aligned with a company's vision and values. These will take center stage, as this breed of individual already probed that learning and mastering a competence is not what makes them unique. From personal experience they have realized that tolerance and broader thinking, they can solve a task with a global personal network. We are not in the era of manufacturing anymore but in the era of creativity and innovation. Hence, a sequential and impersonal way of working where your individual point of view is not part of what you do will become more and more outdated and rejected.

Our life experience has taught us the importance of interlinking visions as way of creating innovation and regional development.

4

Smart cities: what about Mexico?

MARCOS QUINTANA, ENG.*, FRANCISCO
LOPEZ-LIRA HINOJO, ENG.**

*Project Leader at Red Global MX (Netherlands) for the
Tecnológico Nacional de México strategic alliance.
**Founder of Cualli Software B.V. (Spain)

L et us imagine that we could see Earth from outer space in the year 1800. With global population at about 1 billion, there were no extreme pollution problems. The Industrial Revolution was just starting. Imagine that we knew the global population would grow to about 10 billion by 2050. How would we design the human lifestyle to try to maximize standard of living for all, trying to minimize damage to the environment? It is indeed a complex question.

A difficult challenge

It is likely that the global economic model of maximizing profit has been the reason for the extreme growth of urban areas. The estimate is that by 2050 about 68% of the population will be living in cities. This trend requires a dramatic improvement in planning and use of new technologies in city design and management. This article explores some ideas that might be useful in order to understand the *Smart Cities* trend. We explain the case of Mexico in order to emphasize the importance of *smart* planning in the long term. Let us focus in the current situation of the biggest urban areas in Mexico.

The population of Mexico is about 120 million, with about 78% living in urban areas. Mexico has about 120 cities with more than 100 thousand inhabitants. Ten cities have more than 1 million inhabitants. It is estimated that about 30 million people live in the Mexico City Metropolitan Area (referred to as Mexico City hereafter). The UN estimates that Mexico City is the third biggest urban area in the world.

It is obvious that the urban growth of the country has not been optimal. We know that Mexico encompasses an area of roughly 2 million square kilometers with plenty of suitable spaces to design urban areas. As an example, the population density of Mexico City is 2,560 people per square kilometer, while the country has the capacity of bringing that down to just 60. Probably, the most crucial resource to take into account in the design of *Smart Cities* is the long term supply of drinking water. On average, water suitable for human consumption must be brought from a distance of 400 kilometers in order to reach Mexico City, even though it is located 4,000 meters above sea level; it is a complex engineering task indeed. Several of the biggest cities in the north of Mexico grew due to mining industries. Again, the lack of drinking water is a recurrent problem because of their semi-deserted location.

Towards a better life

Pretend that we could reorganize the population of Mexico to achieve better living conditions, *a better life*. In order to do that, let us try to define what *a better life* is. The International Organization for Standardization (ISO) has already worked in this sense and has developed a standard for a holistic and integrated approach to measuring sustainable city development. *The ISO 37120:2014 Sustainable development of communities Indicators for city services and quality of life* defines indicators that allow any city, municipality or local government to measure the quality of life in the community. This standard establishes 100 indicators in 17 categories: economy, education, energy, environment, finance, fire and emergency response, governance, health, recreation, safety, shelter, solid waste, telecommunications and innovation, transportation, urban planning, wastewater, and water and sanitation. Examples of the indicators are: city unemployment rate, total residential electrical energy per capita, particulate matter (PM10) concentration, percentage of women employed in the city government workforce, number of police officers per 100,000 inhabitants, and total domestic water consumption per capita (liters/day).

In Mexico, this standard has already been applied to the city of Guadalajara and the results can be consulted on the World Council on City Data (WCCD) page. Fortunately, there is a recent initiative to apply this standard to more cities: Torreón, Apodaca, Benito Juárez, Campeche, Durango, General Escobedo, Guadalupe, La Paz, León, Querétaro, Toluca, Veracruz y Jalapa. This standard will enable the measurement and assignment of a value to the different indicators, although it will not necessarily lead to improvements. This is where the concept of a *Smart city* can help.

Smart cities

"Smart is as smart does"

To understand what a smart city is (in Spanish *Ciudad inteligente*), we will start with a general definition of *intelligence*, in this case we have selected David Wechsler's definition: *"The aggregate or global capacity of the individual to act purposefully, to think rationally, and to deal effectively with his environment,"* that is, an intelligent being focuses on its **goals** and works towards them **rationally**, taking the **environment** into account. Let's see how it can be applied to a city.

The European Innovation Partnership "Smart Cities and Communities" defines smart cities as: *"systems of people interacting with and using flows of energy, materials, services and financing to catalyze sustainable economic development, resilience, and high quality of life; these flows and interactions become smart **through making strategic use of information** and communication infrastructure and services in a process of transparent urban planning and management that is responsive to the social and economic needs of society"* (the highlight is ours).

There are many initiatives worldwide to work toward a smart city, but here we will analyze five of them: *Songdo* in Korea, *Digital Agenda for Europe*, *The Zeitgeist Movement*, *Mexico City*, *Ciudad Creativa Digital* in Guadalajara, and Smart city Ciudad Maderas.

Songdo

Songdo is a new smart city located in South Korea and built from scratch in 600 hectares. The 10-year project is estimated to cost around $40bn USD. It has been designed to have work, home, school and leisure always within 15 minutes walking distance. Author *Usman W. Chohan* describes the "Ubiquitous City".

The Digital Agenda for Europe

The European Commission (EC) is investing in Information and Communication Technology (ICT) research and innovation to improve the quality of life of citizens and make cities more sustainable. The definition of EC smart city is "a place where the traditional networks and services are made more efficient with the use of digital and telecommunication technologies, for the benefit of its inhabitants and businesses. The smart city concept goes beyond the use of ICT for better resource use and less emissions. It means smarter urban transport networks, upgraded water supply and waste disposal facilities, and more efficient ways to light and heat buildings. And it also encompasses a more interactive and responsive city administration, safer public spaces and meeting the needs of an ageing population".

There are several strategies followed in order to reach the objectives described in the *Europe 2020* Program. The working areas include urban mobility, open data, business models, finance and procurement, policy and regulation, metrics and performance indicators, integrated energy, transport and communication networks.

Zeitgeist

The *Zeitgeist Movement (ZM)* is an organization which goal is the installation of a new socioeconomic model based upon technically responsible resource management, allocation and design through what would be considered the scientific method of reasoning problems and finding optimized solutions. Among the proposals is that of self-sustainably cities. In ZM estimation a city could be designed with current technology to host 50,000 people. The requirement to sustain the city is 100,000 hours being worked a week. In terms of the total population the work responsibility amount to only two hours a week per person.

A few specific city designs could be found in *The Venus Project*. The designs are built in several layers including underground, heating, electric generators, piping systems, recycling systems, basement components, architectural basement. A relevant component is that of ICT in order to optimize resources in the long term.

Mexico City initiatives

Mexico city has some very interesting, although not clearly articulated, ongoing programs related to Smart cities:

The bike-sharing program *Ecobici*, with more than 27 million trips and that has contributed to reduced more than 16 tons. of carbon monoxide since 2010

The *Torre de Especialidades* at Mexico City hospital, under construction, that will neutralize the chemicals present in the smog

The initiative of *green rooftops*, with around 15 thousand square feets of plants

Ciudad Creativa Digital (CCD)

CCD is an initiative under development, located in the historical center of Guadalajara, which aims to concentrate creative industries in a modern and interconnected space. Among its projects are the development of a Data Center, The Ingenium Campus, the rehabilitation of public spaces like Morelos Park or the Alameda Paseo, and an office and co-working space of 27 thousand square meters.

Cd. Maderas Smart city

This is a development project with the goal to create the first Smart city in Queretaro. The project considers to provide information to the settlers on their cell phone of services such as transport, garbage collection , electricity, gas and water. It also considers to have special sensors in homes, that will gather data about moisture, temperature and security alerts. The Internet connectivity will be provided with a fiber optic network that will reach 100% of its inhabitants, hospitals and enterprises.

ICT initiatives in Smart cities

As we saw in the definition of a Smart city, the use of strategic information is one of the pillars and therefore ICT plays a fundamental role. We describe here some applied ICT examples that are currently used in cities. The ideas are useful in order to optimize city resources.

Smart working space

The concept of *Smart Working Space* refers to dynamically booking working rooms or seats for companies and individuals as required. The earlier the reservations are made the easier is to plan and to lower the costs.

This scheme is very convenient for *Work Nomads*, such as independent professionals and visionary/creative/smart companies where connections and contact with others are essential.

The general idea is that the professionals could use the physical working space that is the closest to their location in a particular day.

ICT allows the worker to connect and use a remote desktop or virtual machine where all her information is available from anywhere.

Smart Transport Card

The *Smart Transport Card* is a digital ticket for public transport. The user travels on trains, trams, buses and metros with a single ticket. An example is the *OV-chipkaart* implemented in The Netherlands.

The system allows the user to optimize her transport consumption and to select the billing scheme that better suits her needs. For example, a season ticket for commuting or a discount ticket for off-peak travel.

This system provides a significant amount of valuable information for Transport Engineers which can make better informed decisions to plan new transport designs and to predict behavior when a disruption happens.

Smart waste containers

One of the major problems in the cities is the collection of waste in containers, which requires a careful planning of the route taken by waste trucks every day. This trucks move around the city in a predetermined plan whether the waste containers are full or empty, which sometimes produces unnecessary trips to empty containers or not enough trips to containers that are filled more often.

A solution consists of use wireless sensors to measure and predict the fill-level of waste, which in turn allows the city to make better collection plans with more efficient routes.

Smart Parking

In a typical working day, as much as 30% of the cars could be looking for a parking at the same time, with the consequent waste of time -an average of 30 minutes a day- and the unnecessary emission of CO_2.

The solution adopted for this problem is the installation of sensors in the streets and in parking lots, that detect when a parking space is available and informs the drivers through a signaling system in the streets.

Smart detection of gunshots

If there are gunshots in a city, many citizens will call the police from all areas around where the gunshots were produced, but for the police it won't be easy to specifically locate where the incident happen. And even when they locate a delimited area, they won't be able to tell the origin and direction of the gunshot.

For solving this problems, cities like Chicago, San Francisco, Puerto Rico and Río de Janeiro are installing acoustic sensors all over the city. This sensors are capable of separate the patterns of the sound of a gunshot from other sources of noise and also to estimate the origin of the gunshot and its direction. Although this solution has its own problems, it is very promising.

The following sections describe enabling technologies.

The Internet of Things

The Internet of Things (IoT) refers to the network of things or objects sharing data. This data is sent to be converted into information and then into knowledge, in this way making possible to make better decisions in less time. It is estimated that 30 billion devices will be connected to IoT in 2030 compared to 8.5 billion of people.

IoT is an important enabler technology for Smart cities and it has applications in health sector, energy management, mobility, manufacturing, security and e-government, among others.

Big data

Big data refers to the handling (acquiring, storing and analyzing) of enormous amounts of bytes. It is estimated that every day we produce around 10^{30} bytes. That is, 90% of the data world has been created in the past two years.

With 30 billion devices connected this volume of data will increase meaningfully and we will need special technology and methods to make smart use of it.

Cloud computing

According to Qusay F. Hassan, Cloud computing is a model for enabling ubiquitous, convenient, on-demand access to a shared pool of configurable computing resources. Cloud computing is the third enabler for Smart cities.

Conclusions

The concept of *smart city* should become a part of the agenda of development decision makers in developing countries like Mexico. *Smart Cities* should be planned, constructed and managed with the aim to optimize both environmental preservation and life quality of the citizens. The development of new urban areas should consider ICT as a basic infrastructure element in order to make cities sustainable in the long term.

5
Everybody spread the news!

Social media and citizen involvement as a catalyst
for reshaping society in the next decade

ALEJANDRA RASH*

*Member of Faculty, Autonomous University of
Barcelona. Faculty of Communication Sciences.
Barcelona, Spain.

In my over 15 years of experience as a professional in
the communications field, my interests have brought
me over and over to the world of journalism. My first
job, fresh out of college, was a reporter for a major
newspaper in my hometown city. Back then, at the purest
style of the newsroom where Peter Parker worked, an
overly stressed editor distributed work for all the
journalists. The experienced ones got to cover the "cool"
news, while the newbies, like myself, got to pick up the
work that wasn't interesting to them. Our tools were a
camera, a hand recorder, a pad and a pen.

That was back in 1993. In 2010, after passing through a
series of job positions within the field, from
communications consultant to public relations director, I
found myself again in the world of journalism as the
overly stressed editor-in-chief for an online business
magazine. This time, the newsroom was different, quite
different. Yes, we still had editorial meetings, discussed

the monthly content calendar, the editorial design and distributed work among our writers, but in this occasion, our reporters and journalist were staying in. They had smart phones, tablets, computers and Skype to conduct interviews. In the quiet of their cubicles, they were interviewing on live stream someone in a different city, country or continent. In the newsroom, our reporters were acquiring fresh information out of the prepaid sources on the Web and feeding the live stream of news through a Content Management System (CMS). Social media outlets such Facebook and Twitter, provided instant feedback to our content, and an army of interns not older than 20 were chatting live with our readers and creating email lists, where our readers got feed e-newsletters weekly. Google analytics were our main source of information to direct the content of our publication. There were no printers, nor waiting time to print the next day's edition; content was produced and delivered instantly through a series of sophisticated IT equipment, that in reality didn't appear so sophisticated to us, because it was our everyday work tool. However, for a newsroom veteran, the evolution of the IT's has completely modified and changed, forever, the way we produce, distribute and sell information.

As a professor I found myself teaching courses on "How To Write for News and Public Relations in the Digital Era". Even if the essence of journalism will always be based on the same principles, now we need to teach the importance and downfalls of social media platforms, as well as the importance of analytics, keywords, search engine optimization and CMS management, among others, as basic tools of information production.

When I was invited to participate in this project, I thought to myself, I won't talk about how the IT's have changed the way journalism is made in this day and age. Rather, I'll talk about how the IT's and in particular social media is changing the society, the ways society is doing, thinking and organizing.

In this brief manuscript, I would like to offer my vision about this topic and to do so, I'll use four examples of social mobilization promoted due to awareness brought through social media to specific issues, in hopes to understand to what extent social media and citizen involvement can act as a catalyst to reshape society in the next decade.

The Arab Spring

The Arab Spring originated in Tunisia on December 2010. It is believed that what ignited the movement was an encounter between a Tunisian citizen and the police. Mohammed Bouazizi, a 26-year-old Tunisian man and the subject of this event, went to the municipal office to file a complaint after police confiscated his cart and beat him because he didn't have a permit. It was reported that when ignored by the employers, Mr. Bouazizi set himself on fire in front of the municipal office. Uprisings arose and spread to Egypt, Libya, Syria, Yemen, Bahrain, Saudi Arabia and Jordan.

In 2011, the movement known as the Arab Spring brought the world's attention to a geographical area that used to be somewhat unknown and concealed from the rest of the world. The way social media allowed the world to experience these conflicts spreading and gaining strength throughout the countries of the Arab League and their surroundings was an unprecedented event.

During and after the movement took place, debate about the role that information technology and social media played in the organization and spread of such movement has sparked in scholarly and policy arenas. Generally speaking, there's a notion that while human courage and dignity are the real engine of this movement, social media and communication networks fanned and spread the flames of revolution.

Since that event up to this day, the discussion about how much social media can play a key role in how the society can organize and execute social, political, and economic movements has remained constant, but hasn't quite reached a conclusive point. The British historian AJP Taylor said about the movement, "History reached its turning point, and failed to turn." The truth is that the Arab Spring cannot be credited solely to Facebook; that would be too simple. However, information technology -- satellite television, computer, mobile phones and the Internet-- played a powerful role in informing, educating and connecting people in the region. Many things can still be analyzed from this social, revolutionary movement, but there is an undeniable fact: In this movement, social networks and information technology were used as means to boost, accelerate and increase organization, public interest and support, allowing action by the citizens trying to get back power to the citizens.

#BlackLivesMatter

Alicia Garza and Patrisse Cullors created the hashtag "#BlackLivesMatter in 2012, after the acquittal of George Zimmerman in the Trayvon Martin trial4. Zimmerman, a vigilante from a Florida community, shoot dead an unarmed African-American 17-year-old Trayvon.

Upon hearing the outcome of the trial, Alicia Garza, a long time activist and active precursor of minorities rights in the San Francisco/Oakland area, wrote a letter on Facebook to her community and friends declaring that they must not lose hope, and ending it by saying that her life mattered, her friends' lives mattered, all lives mattered, and black lives mattered. Patrisse Cullors took this opportunity and created the hashtag #BlackLivesMatter. The hashtag immediately gained strength in social media conversations about racial issues.

The hashtag was brought from Twitter and Facebook to the streets after another African-American unarmed teen, Michael Brown, was killed by a white police officer in Missouri, USA. In a march organized through social media on August 30 2014, more than 400 African-American citizens and supporters from different states protested against these events5. The protest attracted the attention of national and international media outlets and soon its coverage was spread throughout the world. The movement quickly gained the support of cultural workers, artists and designers who helped created its own online platform, providing the means to share stories, connect with other likeminded people, but also promoting offline meetings to discuss community issues and plan and execute rides, marches and sit-ins.

This event turned out to be a catalyst to mobilize a new web of civil rights protests in the USA. People have taken the streets in New York, Ferguson, Mo., Cleveland, North Charleston, S.C., and in Baltimore following other cases of unarmed black men and an actual child being injured or killed by police.

#BlackLivesMatter appeared in an episode of "Law & Order: SVU" a TV drama currently in its 17th season that has been sold to over 250 territories around the world and has over 15 million viewers. But probably the most notable attention the movement has received has happening during the current presidential race in the USA. Protestors favoring the movement have appeared at rallies of Democratic candidates for the presidency -- Bernie Sanders, Hillary Rodham Clinton and Martin O'Malley6. In the months since protesters began showing up, they have met with Clinton, and these three Democratic candidates have acted, to some extent, as influential political allies. The hashtag was brought into the Democratic candidates' debate, televised by CNN with an audience of over 13 million viewers.

The movement may have started with a simple Facebook post from a social organizer and activist, but this movement jumped from social media outlets to a very real arena where social discussion and organization is happening. Black Lives Matter currently has 27 chapters in 16 states around the USA and one more in Canada7. It works on a membership basis and organizes events, panels, twitter chats, teach-ins and direct actions around the country. Some sources report that there are conflicts at the core of the movement. There are internal fights and disagreements about who the movement's leaders are and disputes about tactics, but there are also agreements. At the end of the day, the movement that started as a simple hashtag trending on Twitter, Tumblr and Facebook to address social and inequality issues, has grown into an ideological and political intervention.

Ice Bucket Challenge

Amyotrophic lateral sclerosis (ALS) disease was internationally known when it ended the career of baseball player Lou Gehrig, a New York Yankees baseball player, in 1939. In that year he was diagnosed with ALS, a progressive neurodegenerative disease which causes the muscular motor functions to degenerate, resulting in paralysis and ultimately death. ALS is commonly known as Lou Gehrig's Disease.

The ice bucket challenge—a long known challenge originally used by golf players to raise funds for pet charities -- launched by the ALS Association began with Pete Frates, a former baseball player at Boston College, who passed the idea of the challenge to his former teammates and other Boston-area athletes.

The mechanics of the challenge were to dump a bucket of ice cold water on the head while video recording the moment, post the video to Facebook, Instagram, or another social media site and challenge three people to do the same within 24 hours; if they refused the challenge, then they should donate $100USD to the ALS association. The challenge was noticed and covered by the local media and started going viral on social media.

A number of well-known names have taken the challenge, from politicians to athletes to actors and actresses, allowing the challenge to make numerous rounds in social media outlets. According to The New York Times, between June1 and August 13, 2014, people shared more than 1.2 million videos just on Facebook, and it was mentioned more than 2.2 million times on Twitter, according to those sites9. Wikipedia states that after the challenge went viral, public awareness and charitable donations to ALS soared. The site states that hits to an article about ALS on its English site grew from an average of 163,300 views per month to 2.89 million views in August 2014. In a press release one can find on the ALS association webpage, it is stated that between July 29 and August 29, 2014, the Association received $100.9 million in donations compared to $2.8 million during the same period in 201311. It is believed that the Ice Bucket Challenge raised $220 million for ALS Association.

In the same press release, Barbara Newhouse, CEO of the ALS Association, mentioned that the funds will be used "to fund cutting-edge research as well as care and support to people living with the disease..."

However, the ALS Ice Bucket Challenge has faced lots of criticism. Many people, including celebrities, have express their discontent about it, saying that ALS is rather a rare disease and there are many other foundations and associations that can better use those founds. Many others have criticized the movement by stating that while it created a viral phenomenon on social media, it in fact brought very small awareness to what ALS is. Some others, have expressed discontent on several other fronts, from water conservation issues to concern about the excess of funds for an association that was doing just fine with the donations it was receiving before the social media attention. In response to the critics, Newhouse states that the visibility that the disease got as a result of the challenge has brought people to engage in the fight to find a cure for ALS. According to the USA Food and Drug Administration (FDA), in 2014 there was only one FDA-approved drug for ALS and according to the association, the drug can only extend survival by several months.

Steve Perry, director of the ALS Therapy Development Institute in Cambridge, Ma, reported in June 2015 that his lab, among "many others worldwide" received $4 million and that money has allowed researchers of the institute to fund two new drugs for human testing in a matter of months. Perrin's program initially capped at 25 patients, now is planned to include 300.

Reviewing the numbers above stated, one can understand that social media has proved to help raise awareness and funds for this association, but there are many other numbers that prove that social media is a means that could be extraordinarily powerful for charities, however not controllable. Not everyone who participates in this type of social media movements will donate, not everyone who donates will donate again, but the amount of extra money and publicity is, in the end and without a doubt, a benefit for the charities.

Edward Snowden

The American computer professional, former United States National Security Agency (NSA) employee and former government contractor is recognized by some as a hero, while for others he's a traitor. On June 2013, Snowden leaked classified information from the NSA to journalists Glenn Greenwald (The Guardian, UK), Laura Poitras (Producer and Cinematographer), and Ewen MacKAskill (The Guardian's defense and intelligence correspondent)14. The documents revealed information about numerous global surveillance programs, including "Five Eyes" (FVEY) and PRISM.

FVEY refers to an intelligence alliance comprising five countries, including the USA, bound by a treaty for joint cooperation in signals intelligence. After the World War II and through the ECHELON surveillance system, the FVEY was focused on monitoring the communications of the former Soviet Union and the Eastern Bloc. After 2001, as part of the efforts in the ongoing war on terror, the

FVEY expanded their surveillance capabilities, placing emphasis on monitoring the World Wide Web.

PRISM is a surveillance program under which the NSA collects internet communications from major internet companies in the USA, under the Foreign Intelligence Surveillance Act (FISA). There are allegations that the FISA Court had been ordering Verizon Company (a telecommunication subsidiary) to turn over NSA logs tracking all of its customers' telephone calls. PRISM is believed to be the main source of raw intelligence used for NSA analytic reports.

Stories covering the material Snowden revealed initially appeared in The Guardian and The Washington Post, giving him and the issue international attention. Other newspapers published further stories on the subject, including Der Spiegel and The New York Times.

In March 2014, Edward Snowden appeared, through a bot controlled somewhere in Russia, on a TED talk to discuss his actions and their relevance. He said that while working for the NSA, he "saw a lot of things ... that shouldn't be done. Decisions that were being made in secret without public's awareness ... consent, and without even our representatives in government having knowledge of these programs17." Among these "things" that he got knowledge of, he mentioned the PRISM program which "is a program through which the government could compel corporate America, it could deputize corporate America to so its dirty work for the NSA18." He then went on talking about how conversations are tampered and information is mined and harvested in illegal ways violating people's privacy rights.

Reactions to Snowden's actions have polarized public opinion. For some, like the Director of National Intelligence, James Clapper, who declared on June 9, 2013, that Snowden's actions have done a "huge, grave damage19," Snowden is a traitor, while for Sir Tim Berners-Lee, founder of the world wide web, he is a hero20.

Chris Anderson, the curator of TED Conference since 2002 said at this conversation that, "George Orwell got it wrong. It is not Big Brother watching us. We through the power of the web, and transparency, are now watching Big Brother."

But, why include Edward Snowden in a manuscript about social media? For one simple reason: because so far, the free access and lack of control by official or unofficial sources, named government, corporations or any group in particular, have allowed social media to be an open, free, democratic forum where public opinion has found a platform of expression and exposure. Regardless of the sentiment one may have towards Snowden's actions, as a journalist, as a communications professional, it is easy to understand what could be the value of what he brought up to light, and somehow, how it encourages an open debate about citizens' rights to privacy and equally important, freedom of expression. Having access to free, open outlets provided by social media, where information can flow freely and globally, opens up a powerful scenario and that is changing the response and engagement of users of these platforms, not only technology experts, but everyday users, common citizens. Journalism is and will continue to be an important source of news and information, however, the established mass media will not necessarily continue to be the sole holder of the power of information.

Social media outlets may be on their way to balance the power traditional outlets have over the dominium of producing and disseminating content.

Conclusions

"Anything in society can be disrupted with a simple idea".

Recently Don Tapscott, a recognized thinker on innovation, media, and the economic and social impact of technology, launched a $4 million research study on youth, innovation and the collaborative workplace with subjects from Canada and USA. In a TED Talk, he presented his conclusions, and they were not only interesting, but a food for thought. According to Tapscott, the main difference that will shape the next generation from ours will be the fact that the new generations will be born and raised in the digital era, an idea that he's been introducing since 1997 in his books Growing Up Digital.

"The Net Generation," as he called it, "will be comprised of digital native people that will coexist on the basis of four principles that will sustain the open world: collaboration, transparency, sharing and empowerment."

His opinion has been the subject of criticism, but placing his ideas in our actual context, one could see how currently we have a "generational lap24," rather than gap, in technology knowledge. The younger generations are trained and educated in new technology at a very young age. Schools are using information technology to teach basic curriculum and as a working tool, while many members of the older generations were trained, later in life on how to use this technology as a tool of work. This is a substantial generational difference in how we understand and use new IT. The current generation of teenagers understands the properties of open access information, they are used to open collaboration on social networks, where everyone has the opportunity to say what they need to say and access to a myriad of information in, up to some extent, an egalitarian manner.

The Internet seems to be introducing the age of networked intelligence, enabling its users to be producers and disseminators of knowledge and information, where there's leadership, but there's no one leader. It seems to provide a sense of independence based on the interests of the collective. These properties have allowed social movements to spread and gain strength and visibility, and on many occasions, achieving successful results that have jumped from the virtual world to tangible results. It seems like self-organization may have found a powerful new tool in social media.

Did social uprisings happen before social media as we know it? Absolutely. But since their origins, forms of social media and information technology have been involved in the education and dissemination of information. As an example, one can read Greg's Satell's article in Forbes magazine on how in 2004 Kiev, electronic media such online chat boards and mobile phones played an important role in social mobilization25.

I believe that social media, information technology and citizen involvement will serve as catalysts to reshape society in the next decade. I believe a new generation born and raised in the digital era will have a different mindset over control, production, and sharing of information, because they will be used to the practice of sharing and accessing information and knowledge in virtual environments where everyone can express their opinions, but can also be called out on the basis of lack of transparency or veracity. They will be used to living in an environment where collaboration is seen as a means of empowerment and hopefully, this new mindset, given by the way social media and information technology is shaping the practice of how we collaborate as a collective, will result in the knitting of an interconnected world where globalization will take the functional form of a new tangible reality, not only a virtual reality.

References

1 http://www.sourcewatch.org/index.php?title=Arab_Spring

2 http://content.time.com/time/magazine/article/0,9171,2050032,00.html

3 http://www.albanyassociates.com/notebook/2012/03/the-arab-spring-and-the-impact-of-social-media/#_ftn1

4 http://blacklivesmatter.com/

5 How Black Lives Matter moved from a hashtag to a real political force

https://www.washingtonpost.com/news/the-fix/wp/2015/08/19/how-black-lives-matter-moved-from-a-hashtag-to-a-real-political-force/

6 http://www.cbsnews.com/news/democratic-debate-do-black-lives-matter/

7 https://en.wikipedia.org/wiki/Black_Lives_Matter

8 http://www.imdb.com/name/nm0311801/bio

9 http://www.nytimes.com/2014/08/18/business/ice-bucket-challenge-has-raised-millions-for-als-association.html?_r=0

10 https://en.wikipedia.org/wiki/Ice_Bucket_Challenge#cite_note-ALS0829-72

11 http://www.alsa.org/news/media/press-releases/ice-bucket-challenge-082914.html

12 Idem

13 https://als.net/docs/pdf/ibc/resources-and-printables/Drop-in-the-Bucket.pdf

14 https://en.wikipedia.org/wiki/Edward_Snowden

15 https://en.wikipedia.org/wiki/Five_Eyes

16 Idem

17http://www.ted.com/talks/edward_snowden_here_s_how_we_take_back_the_internet/transcript?language=en

18 Idem

19 https://en.wikipedia.org/wiki/Edward_Snowden

20http://www.ted.com/talks/edward_snowden_here_s_how_we_take_back_the_internet/transcript?language=en

21 Idem

22 http://www.thefeministwire.com/2014/10/blacklivesmatter-2/

23 http://dontapscott.com/2012/07/tedglobal-2012-four-principles-for-the-open-world/

24 Idem

25 If You Doubt That Social Media Has Changed The World, Take A Look At Ukraine
http://www.forbes.com/sites/gregsatell/2014/01/18/if-you-doubt-that-social-media-has-changed-the-world-take-a-look-at-ukraine/

6

Is Mexico ready for electric/hybrid vehicles?

PABLO MENDOZA VILLAFUERTE, PH.D.*

*Business Development Manager at AVL in Italy, former Researcher at the European Commission Joint Research Centre Ispra, Institute for Energy and Transport, Sustainable Transport Unit, Ispra, Italy

As Mexico is slowly entering the electrical vehicle revolution, this article focuses on the need to understand the difficulties imposed by the use of electrical/plug-in hybrid vehicles and describes the approach required when planning the implementation of an electrified automotive fleet in a city or town. It also explains the importance of having a coordinated approach between the manufacturers, government, infrastructure and users in order to have an efficient electric vehicle market.

After analyzing a number of initiatives ran in countries like Germany, Czech Republic, Ireland and Italy, the author describes the lessons learned and the benefits of a careful research and understanding of the different factors that electrification and the use of electrical vehicles assert to a city. It also provides some recommendations on the strategy to follow.

Background

The automotive world is changing. Today, the trend to become a society which lives and works in a more efficient way is drawing the path to a better use of the resources that provide us with the energy needed to support the many devices, utensils and means of transport of our daily routine. These factors in conjunction with the growth in population, countries like China, India and the South American region which are booming and slowly evolving to major energy consumers are increasing the amount of oil based fuels used exponentially.

This is becoming one of the main drivers for alternative energy sources technology development and the use of this alternative energy to power those devices. Many countries have consider these difficult scenarios and they have been working on different policies to implement the available technologies accordingly, the European plan is based on their White paper on transport (European Commission, COM(2011) 144 final), in which they illustrate the vision towards the future of the European mobility; the USA has released its Climate Adaptation Plan (U. S. Department of Transportation, 2012), which also enlist a number of action trends and delineation of new policies towards strategic goals on climate change including transport.

Mexico has the Plan Nacional de Desarrollo (Gobierno de la Republica, 2013), which describes the need to contribute towards the reduction of pollutants through the use of efficient fuels, sustainable mobility programs and the elimination of inefficient support to fossil fuel users. The common ground of many of these policies not only reflects the concern on the efficient energy usage but also the environmental and health issues related to high amounts of emissions produced by the automotive fleet.

The polluting emissions of the automotive fleet are increasing as the automotive fleet increases in any city, town or country worldwide. Many technologies have been introduced and implemented in the internal combustion engines (ICE) through the last 30 years (Reitz, 2013); improvements have been made in auxiliary engine systems, air conditioning systems, transmissions and pumping losses, all of which have been directed to make the ICE's more efficient (Berggren, 2012); moreover, important new after-treatment technologies like Selective Reduction Catalyst (SCR) to reduce nitrogen oxides, or Lean NOx Traps (LNT) are now widely used on Euro 6/VI (Euro 6 - Light duty vehicles, Euro VI-Heavy-duty vehicles) certified vehicles. The reduction on transport related emissions has not been as large as many researchers thought, in fact, after the implementation of emissions policies which were based on a standard cycle and that grew from Euro I to the current Euro V, it has been noted that as robust as this approach was thought to be, many manufacturers found the way to make the vehicles behave on a certain way while being tested on this specific cycle and behave differently while outside it (Pelkmans, 2006).

This situation paved the way to the implementation of Euro 6 legislation to what currently is being developed and named as Real Drive Emissions (RDE) voted and approved by the European Member States in April 2015. RDE is possible through the use of Portable Emissions Measurement System (PEMS) (Mamakos, 2013), which will allows to test the vehicles under random cycles of on-road usage to get real emissions data of their performance.

Further to this, on the conclusions of their report on the comparison between the emissions produced by 12 light duty diesel and gasoline vehicles of different sizes comprising of vehicles that were homologated to Euro 3-5 emissions limits, Weiss et al. (Weiss, 2011), concluded that each and every vehicle exceeded substantially their respective Euro 3-5 emissions limits.

The constraints imposed by the new legislation have motivated many manufacturers and universities to work in the resurgence of a technology that enjoyed considerable popularity during the latter years of the nineteenth century and the first couple of decades of the twentieth: the electric vehicle (EV).

Electric and hybrid vehicles are defined in Legislation ECE 101-01 (United Nations, 2011) as: (i) "Pure electric vehicle": means vehicle powered by an electric power train only, where "electric power train" refers to a system consisting of one or more electric energy storage devices (e.g. battery, electromechanical flywheel or super capacitor), one or more electric power conditioning devices and one or more electric machines that convert stored electric energy into mechanical energy delivered at the wheels for propulsion of the vehicle; (ii) "Hybrid electric vehicle": means a vehicle powered by a hybrid electric power train, where "hybrid electric power train" refers a power train that, for the purpose of mechanical propulsion, draws energy from both of the following on-vehicle sources of stored energy/power.

Electric vehicles are becoming one of those fields of study in which many opportunities have arisen through the need of finding a solution to a bigger issue: the awareness of adverse impacts of transport which is highlighting their significant economic, social and ecological costs. Due to this awareness, the concept of electrification of the automotive fleet has gained a good level of support especially on the political arena.

On this note, a careful understanding on what "electrification of the automotive fleet" really means for a city or town has to be reviewed in detail. This article will analyse and highlight the importance of a careful planning on the implementation of an electrified automotive fleet for a city or town. The relevance of this is to support the policy makers and government officials on making educated decisions when it comes to push green agendas which not necessarily will have the desired outcome, resulting on extra costs or inefficiencies which may eliminate future opportunities for development.

Sustainability and transport, can these concepts be related?

The transport industry worldwide has always been a significant contributor to the amount of pollutants in the atmosphere. Vehicles propelled through internal combustion engines use fossil based fuels and additives which produce gaseous pollutants such as CO, CO_2, NOx, THC and particulate emissions.

The amount of pollutants created by the automotive fleet worldwide is responsible for about a third of the greenhouse gases (GHG) existing in our atmosphere. Figure 1 and 2, show the European trend on emissions for two of the most important and critical pollutants: NOx and particulate matter (PM). The transport industry has been running on fossil fuel for the past 110 years; it took several years to understand that the constant growth on population, the growth on the vehicle usage and the decrease on the known sources of fossil fuel to begin thinking on alternative sources of fuel or alternative means to propel the automotive vehicles.

Until then, sustainability and means of transport were two very far apart concepts. With the turn of the century and through the recognition that the known reserves of fossil fuel were limited, the industry began to turn around to technologies that were being explored but not thoroughly thought to be options to the ICE, this trend may change though; recent developments and findings on the possibility of using shale gas and innovative but risky methods to extract oil from the ground have given a breath of fresh air to the industry.

However, many countries are currently looking to find new ways to reduce their fuel consumption and their greenhouse production through implementation of green policies. On this topic Mexico has the following challenges:

Awareness and education on current environmental and energy situation. Sustainable transport technologies: understanding which of these technologies will be relevant to the Mexican situation and could potentially be implemented; sustainable transport policies which will support the implementation and will fund these activities.

On the specific issue of electric and hybrid vehicle deploy in the country, the following issues need to be addressed:

Current Mexican circumstance towards awareness of electrical vehicles. Will electric vehicles could be a factor in diminishing high pollutant emissions concentrations in Mexican cities? Is there any urban research on the viability of electric vehicles on Mexican cities or towns? Are Mexicans aware of the charging and utilization requirements and constraints of electric vehicles?

Federal and Local government challenges. Are cities ready for electric vehicles? Are there plans for infrastructure development to accommodate charging points? Electrical vehicle bays not existent; Are tax incentives for electric vehicles available?

Safety. No safety protocols to deal with damaged electric vehicles

Scientific. There are no electric vehicle technologies being developed in Mexico. Mexico is a manufacturer of these vehicles for export markets. No plans on business related to the electric vehicle due to lack of knowledge of opportunities areas.

Coming back to the topic, the research towards alternative means of traction for vehicles has exploded globally. Many countries have decided to implement programs to further accelerate the development and enhancement of different technologies which will aid on lowering the current emissions levels produced by our transport means. More than 90 projects (ERTRAC, 2013) have been launched within the European green cars initiative which has been supported by the framework program (FP7).

Sample programs

Futur-e-motion (CEZ, 2013): this was an e-mobility project from the Czech Republic in which the Czech energy utility company (CEZ) started a program to test up to a 100 electric Peugeot © in 2010. This program also covered: support of research and development (R&D) and use of new technologies in generation, distribution and consumption of electrical energy, and enabling the customers to monitor and change their energy consumption patterns.

Germany: Several programs have been run in this country supported by Vattenfall©, some of them are the following: Mini E Berlin, Gesteuretes Laden, Pilot Region Berlin (BeMobility), Pilot Region Hamburg (hh=more), etc. The focus is not only on charging units but on how the grid is affected (Vattenfall, 2013).

MeRegio (EnBW, 2013): Project ran by EnBW©, focused on creating a model through the use of 1000 EVs virtually interconnected to develop a market platform for new energy products and services. Specific objectives are related to the billing system, interoperability between different suppliers, cross-border roaming, new energy telematics system all based on user behavior.

Ecars (ESB, 2013): Project ran by the Irish energy company ESB©, their objective is to roll-out 3500 smart charge points, but also to develop the market for providers and software platforms to intercommunicate the charging system with the vehicles.

Having mentioned these programs, it is important to highlight that in all of the initiatives mentioned above, the objective was to study and understand how EVs would interact with the user and the city, there are number of cities in Mexico in which it could be very interesting to run comprehensive studies like the ones ran in Europe, for example, mid-size cities like Queretaro, Puebla, Zacatecas, etc.

Further to the research mentioned above, some other programs have focused on different aspects with the intention to push on alternative means of mobility to obtain further support from the end users; one of such studies was made in Germany. Achtnicht et al. (Achtnicht, 2012) produced a report in which the willingness to pay to reduce the CO_2 was the main topic with a fundamental question: Do car buyers care about the environment?

This is a very interesting subject as it leads us to another question which is: How much are car buyers willing to pay for emissions reductions? This is not a minor topic. Achtnicht et al. concluded that most of the people surveyed were not ready to assume a major cost increase on a vehicle even if it promised to reduce emissions by 30%, willingness to pay is the big question. Hence we are looking at the cultural and economic aspect of a country and a city. The situation for Mexican buyers is not different; according to recent studies (Nielsen, 2014) Mexican car buyers based their decision on emotional motivation and finance capability, placing the electric vehicle in a niche market.

The environmental culture awareness in Mexico currently is being led mainly by NGOs, the government is running environmental programs which have created awareness in terms of the amount of concentrations of pollutants (Gobierno del Distrito Federal, 2013) at a specific day or time of the day, but this awareness has been mainly reactive and consequence of inefficient urban planning and management. The current situation in many Mexican cities calls for definitive action on definition and implementation of strategies to control the high levels of pollution with initiatives that are viable for the citizens and are affordable for the councils.

Speaking about the economic impact of the implementation of alternative technologies and the cost of ownership, the electric vehicles are more expensive than ICE vehicles. This is a fact, and the price will hardly go below the current levels until there are different battery technologies which will lower the overall cost of the vehicle reducing it to more reasonable tier. In order to have a sustainable population of EVs in any city of any country, there are some factors that have to be taken into account, like the cost of the infrastructure that will have to be in place for the vehicles to be able to be charged, cost of ownership if the vehicle is going to be charged at home, maintenance and battery lifespan, etc. The battery lifespan is another issue and its currently forecasted to be 5 years (Lunz, 2012).

Having mentioned some of the costs related to the ownership of EVs, a study on the market of these vehicles and the target population has to be made; this will directly relate to some of the World Bank (World Bank, 2013) indicators like the GDP and the GNI.

On another subject, but again, of outmost importance on the implementation of the EVs in any city, the study ran by Paffumi et al. (Paffumi, 2013) and performed by the European Commission, was to understand the relevance and possible usage of electric vehicles (including hybrid and plug-in hybrid vehicles) through the analysis of mobility requirements in the city of Modena, Italy. This study contemplates the urban mobility of the vehicle fleet through the analysis of huge amount of data generated by vehicles from private users. The data is obtained through a program ran in Europe by the insurance companies; the insurers sell a global positioning system (GPS) through which they obtain information on the mobility of the vehicle. This information is treated as anonymous and is analysed in order to understand the vehicle flux on specific hours, days, months, etc.

The outcome of this important study contains an analysis which highlights the potential of EVs to meet the urban drive needs of the mid-size province. It details the percentage of vehicles moving at one time, shows the peak hours, average parking duration and average speed. It concludes with the assessment of the ability of six types of EVs and four different charge strategies to meet real urban mobility needs.

This means, that before introducing charging infrastructure into this city, this type of information will aid on the process to define the best points to locate the charging points, the number of charging points required by the users, the time frame in which the vehicles will possibly be charged, and the amount of time that the users are going to be parked in one place or another. But maybe the most important point made by this study was the usability of an EV on a city with specific characteristics, demography and weather conditions. All of these factors are crucial when defining the budget of implementation of EVs in any city.

Integrated approach to electrification of the automotive fleet

When talking about the implementation of any new technology in an urban system, one must think about all the sides on which this new feature will affect the rest of it.

The following is a description of the topics needed to be confronted by the different stakeholders on the implementation of the electric vehicle fleet in any city or town. As it can be seen from Figure 3, it is important to include everybody in the planning of the strategy in order to have a successful execution.

The stakeholders on the implementation of EVs and some of the issues that these stakeholders should be addressing:

Users

Is there a need for EVs?

Is there an understanding of the ownership of an EV?

Will users living in flats be able to own an EV? Are real estate developers aware of the requirements for EVs charging?

Users will require education and awareness.

Users will require basic training on high voltage machinery.

Who will use these vehicles?

Where are they going to be used?

In which circumstances are they going to be used?

What type of charging cord and press are the users going to be able to use at home and at public stations?

Infrastructure

Are there any business models available to follow in order to have an efficient program for infrastructure implementation?

What kind of charging points are needed? Fast charging points?

Are there enough charging points available for the users? How many charging points are enough?

Does special electrical vehicle bays are going to be used?

Where do these charging points have to be positioned?

What is the level of usage that these charging points are going to be exposed to?

What is the most efficient way to install the charging points?

How do the charging points will affect the electrical grid?

Any health and safety concerns which needs to be considered?

How can the charging points be accessed?

Who is going to maintain the charging points?

Government:

Based on the usage and requirements of the charging point installation, where are they going to be located?

Is the government going to donate the electric vehicle bays?

Are there going to be any tax incentives on owning an electrical vehicle?

How much do the electrical vehicles will cost to the city and how does this cost will be recovered? How the introduction of these vehicles can be budget neutral?

Is the city prepared to deal with incidents regarding electrical vehicles? Safety and training of the emergency services must occur prior to any electric vehicle hitting the roads.

Are hybrids going to be exempt of programs like those in big cities that prevent vehicles on circulating one day per week?

Energy company

What are the implication of having charging stations on public places?

Where can the charging points be installed based on the requirements needed for its installation?

How the energy is going to be charged to the user?

What security is required around the electric vehicle charging bays?

Can the users charge their vehicles without further installations at home?

What type of charging stations are required? Slow/Fast charging?

Is the grid prepared to absorb the level of demand which will be created by the vehicles that will require charging?

Is the grid prepared to allow energy into it from external sources like the vehicle?

If a special installation is required at home, does the electrical company subsidise this?

Smart Technologies

How can the user interact with the vehicle?

Can the user be able to identify with an application where is the nearest charging station?

Is there an application which will allow the user to pay their consumption by internet?

Can the user be aware when a charging point is not working, or is occupied?

Lessons learned

After analyzing some of the programs and reading some of their reports on performance and recommended actions, there are a few suggestions that have to be considered (Kneeshaw, 2010):

As demonstrated by most of the projects ran in Europe, close cooperation between stake holders is the key for a successful deployment of electric vehicles.

Battery driven vehicles are especially well fitted for small cities; this is due to the short distances to be covered. Through studies like the one from Paffumi et al. (Paffumi, 2013) urban mobility can be analyzed in any city, this is a great advantage and has to be considered as the base for any strategy.

Challenge is to create new business models, partnerships and marketing approaches which integrates EVs to the urban landscape of the city. Cities like London or Milan have congestion charge areas which allow EVs to circulate free within the city center, this is already a benefit compared to the normal vehicles, and a full week of allowance to drive in Mexico City can already be considered an incentive.

Manufacturers are waiting for cities to develop infrastructure and for governments to offer tax allowances and subsides which will make the EVs more attractive to buyers.

Hybrid electric cars are being developed by all manufacturers; this means that they have seen value on directing their research and development to sustainable transport systems, almost every car manufacturer will have a hybrid available within the next 3-5 years. Although this is good news in terms of market availability, the challenge here is to make the batteries more efficient, there has to be a breakthrough which will allow mass manufacturing hence lowering the battery costs. The EVs common current range varies between 100-200kms.

Manufacturers in Mexico require a better incentive to be pushed to implement their hybrids and EVs in a reasonable price; a good incentive would be to make the emissions legislation more stringent. Europe legislation requires car manufacturers to achieve CO_2 emissions targets. Average CO_2 emissions for the passenger car fleet is 130gCO_2/km by 2015 and 95gCO_2/km by 2020.

Energy and infrastructure suppliers need to be active players in strategies to increase EVs, there will be new opportunities to create, install and maintain the charging points and associated systems.

Many of the programs mentioned above were created and ran by the electric energy companies; this is to say that it is in their own interest to understand how their grid and their business will be affected. The Mexican electrical energy company needs to begin working on these topics. Implementation of EVs not only opens the door to many other possibilities of entrepreneurships on infrastructure, but also on renewable energies and greener transport modes. EVs must be the reason behind the push for renewable energy sources (RES), there are open debates on what percentage the EVs must run on RES.

The use of smart technologies to charge the vehicles, based on a smart charging strategy which will communicate the vehicle with the grid is a promising field for new business opportunities. Any aspect that has to do with the charging side, like: voltage and frequency stabilization during blackouts, balancing power, bi-directional vehicle-to-grid charging, etc., or user interface may be an opportunity to develop new businesses.

Electric vehicles will have a positive impact on the environment ONLY if they replace a significant amount of conventional vehicles. A cultural change is needed, education is key on the efforts to create consciousness about the benefits of using these vehicles. Awareness and education are not equal to merchandising campaigns.

Several schemes can be linked to this new technology, from car sharing schemes to car-pooling clubs.

The aim must be to replace current conventional vehicles with EVs, in Europe more than 80% of the journeys averages below 20km, and Europeans drive less than 40kms in one day; is there an understanding on what these numbers are in Mexico?

Conclusions

In order to have a good idea on how the electrical vehicles fit in the Mexican urban landscape, some research is urgently required. The universities along with experts on these topics need to take the initiative to create the awareness and to thoroughly understand the topics they should be focusing on. These topics must cover all the details to have a successful integration of the infrastructure required for the EVs.

There are many issues that can be addressed prior to have the EVs running in the cities and having to deal with safety, running-out-of battery or parking issues (to name but a few) which good planning can tackle and prevent future headaches.

There must be a good collaboration between the stakeholders in order to have a robust plan, the manufacturers must be very careful on what they offer to the customers, more over because the electrical infrastructure in Mexico may not be as robust as in other parts of the world.

The EVs can be part of the solution to reduce the level of pollution in some of the cities in Mexico, but once starting to define the policies, urban planning and deployment of these vehicles in the cities; this effort can be a god starting point to include other green energy alternatives.

Mexico has a new energetic reform, this reform mainly focuses on the continuity of the search of new fossil based oil reserves, for this, there is a complicated political landscape. Maybe this is a good time to include a good overview of what other sources of energy can be legislated and a way to Mexico re-direct their energy policies. The time to act is upon us, the later Mexico gets grips with electrification the cost will be much higher.

Disclaimer: The views expressed are purely those of the writer and may not in any circumstance be regarded as stating an official position of the European Commission.

References

Achtnicht, M. (2012). German Car Buyers' willingness to pay to reduce CO2 emissions. Centre for European Economic Research.

Berggren, C. M. (2012). Reducing automotive emissions - The potentials of combustion engine technologies and the power of policy. 41, 636-643.

CEZ. (2013). Futur-e-motion Energie. Retrieved from CEZ: http://futuremotion.cz/cs/uvod.html

EnBW. (2013). MeRegio - EnBW AG. Retrieved from MeRegio: http://www.meregio.de/en/index.php?page=partner-enbw

ERTRAC. (2013). European Green Cars Initiative. Retrieved from European Green Cars Initiative: http://www.green-cars-initiative.eu/projects

ESB. (2013). Electric cars, electric vehicles, hybrid vehicles, charge points, charging - ESB ecars. Retrieved from Ecars: http://www.esb.ie/electric-cars/about-esb-electric-cars.jsp

European Commission. (COM(2011) 144 final). White Paper - Roadmap to a soingle European Transport Area - towards a competitive and resource efficient transport system.

Gobierno de la Republica. (2013). Plan Nacional de Desarrollo 2013-2018. Mexico D.F.: Gobierno de la Republica, Mexico.

Gobierno del Distrito Federal. (2013). SMA Programa Hoy no circula . Retrieved from El Portal del programa Hoy No Circula de la Secretaria del Medio Ambiente del Distrito Federal.: http://www.sma.df.gob.mx/hnc/

Kneeshaw, S. (2010). Electric Vehicles in Urban Europe - Baseline Report. URBACT II network.

Lunz, B. Y. (2012). Influence of Plug-in hybrid electric vehicle charging strategies on charging and battery degradation costs. 46, 511-519.

Mamakos, A. B. (2013). Assessment of portable emissions measurement systems (PEMS) for heavy-duty diesel engines with respect to particulate matter. 57, 54-70.

Nielsen. (2014). Secure Tomorrow's car buyers today - Four market strategies that will fuel industry growth globally. Nielsen.

Paffumi, E. D. (2013). Electric Vehicles and charging strategies to meet urban mobility requirements. WIT Transactions on The Built Envirnoment , 533-544.

Pelkmans, L. D. (2006). Comparison of on-road emissions with emissions measured on chassis dynamometer test cycles. Transportation Research Part D (11).

Reitz, R. (2013). Directions in internal combustion engine research. 160, 1-8.

U. S. Department of Transportation. (2012). Climate Adoption Plan. Department of Transport.

United Nations. (2011). ECE 101-01. Emissions of Carbon dioxide and fuel consumption. UN.

Vattenfall. (2013). Research and Development Vattenfall. Retrieved from Vattenfall: http://www.vattenfall.com/en/research-and-development.htm

Weiss, M. B. (2011). Analysing on-road emissions of light duty vehicles with portable emissions measurement systems (PEMS). European Commission.

World Bank. (2013). GDP Per Capita (current US$). Retrieved from The World Bank: http://data.worldbank.org/indicator/NY.GDP.PCAP.CD/countries

7
Books vs eBooks: the Battle for Readers

JIMENA GORRAEZ-BELMAR*

*Marketing and Social Media Manager, Gallic Books & Aardvark Bureau, UK.

A few years ago, when the digital revolution reached our everyday life, there was serious talk about the death of the printed book. All of a sudden books brought with them endless problems: they took space, they were heavy, libraries were a homage to dust and moldy pages, books got wet, pages tear if not careful, books may not fit in a small bags; and when on holidays you cannot take more than two for all the above reasons. The answer was simple: books had to go digital and to achieve that the e-reader was born.

Retail giant Amazon launched Kindle in 2007. In 2010 Kobo arrived along with Nook and BeBook. All of them promising same functionality as Kindle but at a lower price. Today, the only survivors in the e-reader category are Kindle and way behind are Kobo and Nook. Kindle's dominance is so great that in 2012 there were an estimated 17.4 million Kindle Fire users in the United States. To all of this, add the option of downloading the Kindle app into devises such as mobile phones, tablets and computers.

Like never before, the bookselling industry was a click away from reaching an absolute mass audience. People were hungry for books delivered instantly into their devices. Entire libraries were now being kept in a machine which was thinner and lighter than a 50 page novel! Books were now dust and mold free, water proof (as long as the e-reader remained on a dry surface) and for the first time ever a book could be read with the lights off. And adding to all that, eBooks were in average 20-30% cheaper than a physical copy.

While the internet was going crazy with eBooks, the uncertainty of the printed word and specifically the survival of bookshops became evident. In 2011 the UK saw the first casualties as well established bookselling chains *Books etc.* and *Borders* went into administration and closed down. In 2014, the prestigious *Blackwell's* lost it's flagship store in Charing Cross after 19 years in this once iconic bookselling street.

It is difficult to blame the eBook frenzy for the loss of high street bookshops. And while *Books etc, Borders* and *Blackwell's* chocked, *Daunt Books, Foyles* and *Waterstone's* expanded. For example, in a 5 period of years, Foyles opened new branches including London's South Bank, Westfield Stratford City and Waterloo Station; plus one in Bristol and, most recently, the brand new Birmingham Grand Central station. *Daunt Books* also enjoyed expansion and *Waterstone's* became, without any doubt, the most important UK retailer.

As these independent stores gained strength along with the increasing popularity of eBooks, smaller independent bookshops made their grand entrance. In a time when the printed word was supposed to be in decline, local and privately owned bookshops started appearing. This is the case of shops like West End Lane Books in West

Hampstead, Belgravia Books in well, Belgravia, and Big Green Bookshop in North London to mention only a few.

All of a sudden it seemed there was room for everyone. There was hope that eBooks and printed books could live side by side. But the survival of them both depends on readers. And here is where the battle begins. Let's have a look at it from three different angles: the reader, the bookshop and the publisher.

The reader

There are people like me, who pledged to read only the printed word and eventually couldn't resist the Kindle app on my tablet. And the reason why I broke my promise relies in the fierce battle for readers in which Amazon is advancing with the most powerful army.

Amazon is able to offer mind blowing discounts on books. People love a deal and the opportunity to buy an eBook for less than £1 is almost irresistible. That's why Amazon's promotions are so successful for both: readers and them.

For book lovers, blogs are an invaluable source of information. In the battle for readers, publishers cherish popular and influential book bloggers as they see them as multipliers of information. Set up a blog, be willing to review advanced copies and chances are you'll receive piles of proofs from all sorts of publishers. Bloggers are the new word of mouth, and readers trust the opinion of book bloggers as their approach can be a lot more accessible than literary critics in newspapers, journals or magazines.

As we all know, social media gives the reader the opportunity to interact directly with authors. That sells too. Making authors visible on Twitter, Instagram,

Facebook, Pinterest it's becoming almost essential. And let's not forget the good old 'freebies'. Giveaways such as those offered on sites such as Goodreads and all sorts of competitions, raffles, etc to win free copies are some of the many strategies to win the attention of readers. At the end of the day, word of mouth is still one of the most successful ways of marketing a book. But the first step is to make sure the reader has access to it, regardless of the format.

Bookshops

In this competitive times, bookshops have to offer a personalized service, catering, most of the time, for the area they are in. Small independent shops are becoming well regarded in local communities, and the specific case of bookshops is proven to raise the profile of an area. Pretty much in the same way as having a Waitrose near may help to increase the value of a property.

Bookshops are fascinating places, mainly because 80% of people who walk into them do not know what they want. It is a fact. As they walk around, looking here and there, browsers are more likely to pick up a book because they like the way it looks. Now more than ever, it is important to judge a book by its cover. The time and money invested in designing jackets (as covers are known in the publishing industry) is incredible. At the same time, booksellers play a key role in the battle for readers as they have a direct and immediate power of influence. People who ask a member of staff for a recommendation are very likely to buy the suggested book.

Now, how do bookshops enter the battle for readers under the banner of the printed word? Well, events are the key. What bookshops tend to maximize is the possibility of offering interaction with other like-minded people. Strategies such as meet the author, book clubs and workshops are becoming increasingly popular as they give shops another breath of life by becoming meeting points. And let's not forget the all-important and desired signed copy from best known authors. This may not always increase the value of the book in the long term but it adds to the charms that a book has to offer.

The publisher

As any other industry, making publishing profitable is about selling. And this is a fierce war. They all want to feature in newspapers and literary magazines. For example, a book review (bad or good) in The Guardian, The Times Literary Supplement or The Financial Times means sales. But these reviewers get hundreds of books very week from all sorts of publishers of fiction and non-fiction, paperbacks and hardcopies. All of them fighting for a space that will put them in the spotlight for the other thousands of readers out there.

Then comes Amazon once again. Publishers must list their titles on Amazon to make them visible together with the controversial policy for selling those books, particularly on the eBook market. The method is very straightforward: publishers have little option but to offer Amazon discounts of 70-90% off the retail price. If your book is not in Amazon, it's invisible. As simple as that. Once you have given Amazon a massive discount on your books, they have a little evil laugh and sell eBooks for as little as £0.99p on its Kindle Daily and Monthly Deal.

In order to get there, publishers nominate titles for this kind of promotions, on a monthly basis, hoping to sell loads at a very small price but making some sort of profit.

The idea behind it is that mass selling can get the book into the Kindle best-sellers which will later benefit of sales of the eBook on a non-discounted price (which again is at least 40% to 60% cheaper than the printed version). Companies such as Penguin Random House, Harvill Seckler, Simon and Schuster, etc. by all means make good money when selected in those promotion, but independent small ones may not be so lucky.

In 2008 a very intelligent marketing tool was created in the United States which, in many ways, brings harmony to the existence of eBooks and printed books. It is called NetGalley. Here is how it works. Publishers pay a membership that entitles them to make their forthcoming titles or those in their backlist available on PDF and mobi format (aka Kindle). On the other side, bloggers, librarians, academics, critics, etc. sign up for free and browse either by genre, publisher or simply looking around to see what's available.

To access some titles, publishers have to approve the reviewer but other books are made available by only requesting it. Once this is done, the file gets downloaded into a Kindle devise or app, or as a PDF. The more people review, the more access publishers give to titles not yet published. Reviewers have a points system which keeps the ball rolling and protects the publisher from giving advanced copies for free. A review is expected when a NetGalley user requests and downloads a file.

The wonder about NetGalley is that publishers are able to reach an audience that is genuinely interested in their titles. There is a lot of waste in posting proofs to extensive mailing lists when reviewers or bloggers may simply not be interested. In that respect, NetGalley is incredibly efficient by giving publishers access to a completely new database of people who can effectively market their books by providing honest reviews.

I believe there is room for eBooks and books. Nowadays, a publisher simply cannot escape offering their lists on eBook; but for the reader is simply a matter of choice. I consider myself to be a bit of a 'purist' and will always prefer to read on printed paper. I have tried both formats and I found that my attention spam on an eBook was much more reduced. It also took me a lot longer to read an average length novel, and was unable to pace myself turning virtual pages. Not being able to 'feel' where I was in the book or how close I was to the end did affect my reading experience. Of course, it can be argued that there is an indicator at the bottom of the screen, but for me, didn't do the trick.

There is no doubt that e-readers will develop to be as close to a physical book as possible. However, for those book lovers like me, reading a good book has the valuable input of being able to keep it. Books and their stories can travel with us. Who hasn't opened a book and found a long forgotten postcard or a photograph? Or perhaps a coffee-stained page that remind us of an exact place and time? That is why is perfectly ok to kiss your book goodnight or shed a tear when you turn the last page of a heart breaking story. As any other objects, we attach memories and emotions to books and by keeping them they become part of our lives.

8

The Future of Teaching Film Studies

ARMIDA DE LA GARZA, PH.D.*

*Senior Lecturer in Digital Humanities and Screen Media at University College Cork, Ireland

The future of Film Studies is emblematic of the times the world faces today, namely times of radical transformation. To put it simply, the future of Film Studies as such is to disappear. The largest producer of film stock, Kodak, filed for bankruptcy in 2012. Film is dead (see for instance (Godard, 2011; Gras & Gras, 2000). Hardly anyone makes films anymore, and very few care about studying films in the old way either. The future of cinema and other image-based communication however, is looking digital bright. Indeed, Lev Manovich has famously redefined cinema as 'colors changing in time' (Manovich, 2000, p. 302), since the pixel is the new unit. In the paragraphs that follow, I briefly discuss the main transformations that in my view will drive Film Studies, most probably to be renamed Screen Media, into the future: learning by doing, computer-based teaching and learning, inter and trans-disciplinarity and collaboration. The conclusion briefly summarizes the arguments.

Learning by Doing

As I write these lines, I recall the invitation to contribute to this volume, which clearly stated the network aspires to go from being a 'Think Tank' into becoming a 'Do Tank', that is, a network capable of sparking people into action. I would say the same spirit lies at the heart of the transformation that digital technology has brought into Film Studies, making its future so much more active, engaged and hopefully also community involved and socially relevant. In the old days, you learned to make films in Film School. Film Studies was about film criticism. Film School was practical, vocational, all about doing. Film Studies was about thinking, theory, history, and writing essays. Today however, changes in technology and society more generally have finally made it possible to combine thinking and doing, theory and practice. Whereas only a few could own a film camera in the past, today every student comes with their mobile phone camera, already good enough to make full feature films. Increasingly, more and more students come with informal know-how too, such as having produced and edited their own videos for social media. Thus this is perhaps the first important change, and one that is bound to continue in the future. Film School and Film Studies are merging into *Screen Media*. Students of film no longer watch films made by others to write about them, or even to become critics of culture and society, but can now make their own and use them for expression, business, activism, or any other purpose. Moreover, when they enter university they are already conversant with visual language and familiar with the technology, which gets cheaper and easier to use year by year.

Computer-based Teaching and Learning

The curriculum is already changing dramatically in the light of the approaches that digital tools now afford, and this change will continue in the future. Digital tools today go well beyond early applications in the 2000s that brought together the script, the storyboard and the first frame of each shot of a given film into a full screen, so that a student could, for instance, learn about lighting by changing the lights with the touch of an area of the screen, to see the effects. Those early digital tools, effective as they were, did not so much change the approach to the study of films as facilitate it.

But the old approaches that came out of literature departments and regarded films as texts, concentrating on characters, plot and genre and even considered certain directors as auteurs, or the sociology-based approaches that gave primacy to issues of class, gender, ethnicity and nationality, are giving way to approaches that focus on the image and rely on computer interfaces, geo-spatial positioning systems, big data and data visualizations. For instance, algorithms extract the colors of each pixel in each frame so that their saturation, luminosity and contrast can be calculated. Millions of pixel changes can be calculated in less than a minute. This allows comparisons to be made between different shots in the same film, or between animations made for children and those made for adults, which contribute to studies on the psychology of color (Brunick & Cutting, 2014). Another example is Barry Salt's *Cinemetrics* project (Salt, 2011), a crowd-sourced database that has been collecting information on film shots, their type, duration and frequency, contributing to studies of stylistics and attention. In the future, algorithms as tools and a focus on the image and its materiality that build on projects such as the ones described here are bound to become ever more prominent.

Importantly, digital media has also made a dazzling number of films from all over the world available wherever one might be with the touch of a screen, in some ways making the old film festivals redundant. This is also making the younger generations familiar with a breadth of works from all over the world that would have been impossible even a few years ago, albeit not necessarily the same works. The result is a much more cosmopolitan audience, with a much reduced common background.

Inter and Trans-disciplinarity

The third trend to discuss involves the tendency to collaborate across fields in the humanities and the social sciences, and even to promote collaborations between the arts and natural science more generally. It is already acknowledged that the model of specialization and narrowing down as in the twentieth century has run its course, and that a model that conceives of knowledge as whole and integrated, more after Leonardo Da Vinci, is urgently needed. Some of the most interesting and highly original projects in Screen Media have come out of these inter and trans-disciplinary collaborations. As an example I can mention the digital map that the Department of Communication at the University of Liverpool made for the City of Liverpool Museum in 2011. When users touched an area of the map, such as a park or a street, short clips from films that had been made there between the years 1897 and 1996 appeared on the screen, so that the way the area had changed in all those years could easily be seen. The way the city had slowly transformed came to light together with the actors and actresses that had been famous in those years, and the project also gave access to the lives and worldviews of a variety of amateur film and documentary filmmakers that contributed works. It vividly showed for instance how a school that had been there in the 1920s had become a hospital during the war, only to be demolished in the 1950s. The project thus involved the collaboration of architects, historians, film scholars, the British Film Archives, GPS experts and the community of people who live in Liverpool. It also allowed the teaching and learning of films and film history through GPS technologies, and it produced a long-lasting addition to the City Museum collection, that will be useful to all visitors.

One might think that film scholars and mathematicians would not make for natural research partners, unless it were on a documentary about mathematics. However, collaboration with mathematicians and statisticians has opened up entire new fields to Screen Media (formerly Film Studies). As an example, I can mention the use of Markov chains, defined as a model describing a sequence of possible events in which the probability of each event depends only on the state attained in the previous event. These chains have been used to determine how films could have travelled in a theatre distribution circuit, reconstructing a whole period and the stocks of entire companies on the basis of just a few titles.

But perhaps the most exciting research agendas come from collaborations with the natural science. Film impacts emotion and thus memory. As we watch films, the amygdala is stimulated, which provides emotional rewards. Anxiety induced by horror films moves brain activity to the frontal lobe and thalamus, suggesting arousal. Neurologists have thus been scanning the brains of viewers to learn which paths are triggered by specific stimuli, with huge potential for the use of film as a kind of medicine to assist in the treatment of dementia and other related illness. Other applications have to do with the impact of images of violence on the brain (Wijdicks, 2015).

Again, it is likely that these kinds of collaborations will continue to thrive as they are producing such interesting and important results,[1] leading the way forward where discipline-based research had stalled.

Conclusion

Film Studies was a narrow academic discipline, concerned with the theory-based analysis of a body of films that were primarily in English or made by English-speaking directors/countries (if one wished to study the cinema of any non-English speaking nation it would have come under 'Area Studies' or 'Art Cinema'). Opportunities for employment were thus restricted.

The profound changes that the discipline is undergoing however, mainly brought about by technological advance and broader social developments, are transforming it beyond recognition. In the future, Film Studies will become Screen Media Studies. It will be far more fluid and cosmopolitan. Its students will be knowledgeable in a broad variety of subjects, including coding and software design, in addition to aesthetics, communication, cinematography, and even marketing and management, two of the main sources of employment for graduates already. They will be primarily interested in the digital visual image, including game systems, which in fact will comprise a large part of the new (inter)discipline. They will also be trained to collaborate, to be team players, to contribute to pose much bigger and ambitious questions, and to become adaptable and respond quickly to change.

Screen Media will be a much more practical and diverse field with loose boundaries, centered on transferable skills that will also be useful for life. Ideally this will mean it will be socially engaged and community relevant, offering opportunities for personal, creative expression and growth; for business and professional development; or for participation and persuasion through activism, seeking to move others into action. In short, if in the past Film Studies happily sat in a Think-Tank, Screen Media will proudly move, and even fly, animating the Do-Tanks of the future.

References

Brunick, K. L., & Cutting, J. E. (2014). Coloring the Animated World: Exploring Humn Colour Perception and Preference Through the Animated Film. In T. Nenicelli, & P. Taberham (Eds.), Cognitive Media Theory (pp. 124-138). London: Routledge.

Godard, J. L. (2011, 07 12). Film is Over. What do we do? The Guardian .

Gras, V., & Gras, M. (2000). Peter Greenaway: Interviews (Conversations with Filmmakers). Jackson: University Press of Mississippi.

Hallam, J., & Roberts, L. (2013). Locating the Moving Image: New Approaches to Film and Place. Bloomington: Indiana University Press.

Manovich, L. (2000). The Language of New Media. Cambridge, MA: MIT.

Salt, B. (2011). Cinemetrics. Retrieved 10 11, 2015 from http://www.cinemetrics.lv/metrics_in_cinemetrics.php

Wijdicks, E. F. (2015). Neurocinema: when Film Meets Neurology. London: CRC Press.

---

[1] For more on these and other exciting examples, see (Hallam & Roberts, 2013).

9

Sustainable opportunities to feed 2 billion additional people by 2050

ANA CRISTINA DUTTON TREVIÑO, PH.D.*

Senior R&D Global Specialty Crop Manager at Syngenta Crop Protection Basel, Switzerland.

W e are all aware that the global population is growing. Current FAO estimates are that by 2050 the planet will have 9 billion people. Today that means that approximately 200,000 new mouths per day will need to be fed. But population growth isn't the only reason we'll need more food. The spread of prosperity across the world, especially in China and India, is driving an increased demand for meat, eggs, and dairy, boosting pressure to grow more corn and soybeans to feed more cattle, pigs, and chickens. If these trends continue, this will mean doubling the amount of crops we grow by 2050.

Our global challenges today

In addition, we presently face several issues and concerns regarding agriculture including, 1) the loss of land and biodiversity, 2) the contribution of farming to global warming through the substantial methane released by cattle and rice farms or/and nitrous oxide from fertilized fields, 3) the demand of limited resources like fresh water of which today 70% is used for agriculture,[1] and the related uncertainty of droughts which account for huge crop losses in all continents, 4) the contribution of pesticides and fertilizers pollutants in water sources, 5) the loss of people working in agriculture moving from the rural areas to urban cities.

In the following pages I would like to illustrate that there is no need to increase the acreage of farm land in order to meet the future food requirements, already an important component to stop the destruction of pristine land (i.e. rain forest). Moreover, through new developing technologies in agronomic mechanization and breeding there are many opportunities in which sustainable production can be optimized using integrated solutions to meet the demands in food production. And that education and suitable technology transfer are important components to sustainable growth in agriculture.

Is it possible to increase productivity without using more land?

The answer is probably yes and can be illustrated with the following examples which give an idea on the levels of production that have been reached on two field crop in some parts of the globe and a view on how Vertical Farming₂ is already becoming a reality on increasing production for vegetables in urban space.

Potato: China is today the world's major producer of potato with 5 million hectares of land and plans to have 10 million by 2020. The average production in the country is 17 t/ha, this is far behind the average global yield of 22 t/ha and not even half of the yields obtained in European countries which are around 42 t/ha (in countries where environmental compliance is stringent).

Cotton: A non-food crop, with India having the largest acreage (12.7 million hectares) of land dedicated to the crop and only producing on average 500 kg/ha compared to Australia were 2,000kg/ha are produced.

Vegetables (lettuce): Production in Vertical Farming, one of the first examples of a commercial producer is in Japan, Shigeharu Shimamura's farm, who was able to prove that it is possible to economically produce with 25,000 square feet of area 10,000 heads of lettuce a day which corresponds to 100 times more per square foot than traditional methods. Large scale Vertical Farms are already a reality in different countries, in Singapore there are over 100 towers that stand nine meters tall producing various vegetables for the city´s population.

Some of the big leaps in agriculture and where do we expect major improvements in the future in order to produce more sustainably?

Mechanization

No doubt that several technologies such as the moldboard plow in the 18th century carved a new path for agriculture. Not only was it the first plow to dig soil up but also turned it over, allowing the cultivation of harder ground. The combine harvester in the 1930s in the US was also a significant milestone to food production as part of the Green Revolution where yields of major staple crops were increased and machinery was required in order to harvest more efficiently.

Precision agriculture and digital solutions are changing the way farmers are producing today and will have an important impact on sustainable ways of producing food. In some industrialized countries it is not new for farmers to drive computerized tractors equipped with sensors and Global Positioning Systems (GPS) where pesticide and fertilizer applications are provided according to crop needs reducing excessive inputs to the crop. However, the full potential of precision agriculture is still at an early phase. Here, I will provide a brief example on what some researchers[3] already foresee for the near/middle future on taking advantage of technologies that are being developed in other areas and which can be incorporated into the automated management of pests and optimize crop management. Automated systems will likely have sensors and computer technologies that will be able to categorize plants in the field and identify whether they are crop or weed. Today GPS digital imaging can determine nutrient levels within the crop by using digital canopy color, also digital imaging systems can capture the taxonomic classification of plants however progress is still needed to determine minimal digital resolution to maintain species discrimination. Upon identification of the plant the automated sensors will determine what to do next. If it is a weed then a toolbox of options can take place, for example, application of a micro-rate of herbicide or having a tool to pull out or cut the weed without injuring the neighboring crop. If the identified plant is a crop then micro scale sensors such as those being developed for health and environmental sciences nano-piezoelecronics[4] could be used for identifying the state of the plant. Currently Georgia Tech scientists are working with this technology to study early signs of human diseases in the blood, as well as trace contaminants in food. These potentially could also be used in the future for accessing the health, physiological or stress state of the plant to make further decisions on what actions to take. The most advanced digital systems are probably those currently used in greenhouse grown crops. Already available and in use is the GroNTec5 for pepper growers which provides the grower with remote information regarding the physiological (stress) state of the crop to make decisions on when to apply products in order to maximize plant productivity. One can envision sensors in the future, which can assess if a plant has been attacked by a pathogen, insect or nematode and then take decisions on what product the plant requires.

Today with the available technology it is still too early to monitor the entire field at the individual plant scale and it will require a wide range of specialists working together to refine the tools that will be needed in the future. Success will only be possible through the integration of expertise from the multiple fields including agronomists, chemists, engineers, computational experts, and also breeders which will play a significant role in the future of sustainable production. We must remember that it was the combination of hybrids and fertilizers that made the Green Revolution a success. No doubt that optimizing variety will also be important and we can take a look of what has been achieved until today and what will the trends and needs in the future.

Crop Breeding

Conventional breeding has no doubt allowed for the increase in yields. The Green Revolution marked an important step in bringing hybrids to the field. Hybrids together with the increase in fertilizers were able to double yields. From those days to today there has been a further step and genetically engineered (GE - today called biotech) crops were introduced to the market in 1995. Twenty years after the first introduction of biotech crops there are over 180 million hectares of land planted worldwide with mainly insect (*Bt*) and herbicide tolerant (HT) soybean, corn, cotton and maize. Recent approvals for *Bt* eggplant, Innate™ potato with low levels of acrylamide, an alfalfa event with reduced lignin content and the first drought tolerant maize have been granted.[6] In the initial years it was only the industrial countries (mainly US) cultivating the crops and today the developing countries have overtaken and are leading in the surface area planted with biotech crops. The pros and cons of the technology are still a social, economic and political debate. Questions still remain on their economic and environmental impact. A large portion of the criticism has been that multinational companies introduced the technology and were blamed for generating a monopoly in the seeds and chemical industry. One of the initial introduced traits, herbicide (glyphosate) tolerant crops was developed to be used with the herbicide glyphosate, making growers depend on both products. On the other side NGO's together with the media were able to provide a misleading view of the technology, claiming that GE crops were 'Frankenstein food'.

The question on whether current GE crops have helped to increase yields is still asked. But perhaps the question should be whether the technology has proven to be more sustainable to conventional practices. Last year, the USDA provided an Economic Research Report (number 162)[7] with an analysis of the last 15 years since the adoption in the US. The findings show that with insect-resistant (*Bt*) crops (cotton and corn) there is an increase in yields by mitigating losses due to insects feeding on the crop. Yield benefits of HT crops showed mixed results. However, with the use of both *Bt* and HT crops inputs of crop protection products has mostly decreased reflecting a reduction of pesticides use. Until now no human or environmental risks have been associated with the cultivation of biotech crops and after 15 years in the field the main concerns are related to the development of insect and weed resistance which is related and expected remarkable ability of pests to adapt to pest control technologies. This in fact is not different to what we have observed through history with conventional pesticides. And this clearly reminds us that adopting one technology for solving a pest will never succeed. Producing in a sustainable manner will require integrated solutions where different technologies are combined.

Obviously biotech crops are now well established and there is an enormous potential for the future. The speed at which molecular and genetic research is moving has allowed that transformations are no longer trans-genic (genes from one organism inserted into another organism), as has been the case for the current commercial events, but transformations are cis-genic (resistance genes which have been identified in a wild species are transferred to the same commercial species). Moreover, the transformations are no longer done with the assistance of Agrobacterium or by using the gene gun where controlling the insertion of the DNA into the crop was half hazard. Today new methods including zinc finger nucleases (ZFN), technology clustered regularly interspaced short palindromic repeat (CRISPR) and transcription activator-like effector nucleases (TALENs) are successfully being used for the precise introduction of DNA to allow for maximum gene expression.

There are two exciting things happening today with the development of biotech. On one side the clear recognition that integrated solutions are a key to success in sustainable resistance management. An excellent 10 year public research conducted in Wageningen University under the name DuRPh-Durable Resistance against *Phytophthora* illustrates this. The project´s aim was to develop different potato varieties resistant to late blight (the pathogen that caused the Great Famine in Ireland in 1845) and establish a late blight resistance monitoring tool as well as the 'no spray unless needed' strategy. The insights on the pathogen population, the need for several stacked genes in potato and the possible need and acceptance of fungicide applications to ensure that resistance is managed in a sustainable manner illustrates that there has to be a holistic understanding of the crop and pest in time and space. The second exciting thing is the evolving Public Private Partnerships which have been established within the last few years to help in specific crops which have less commercial value but where today there are no efficient environmentally safe solutions available. The first of these partnerships was one between Mexico biotech lab CINVESTAV in conjunction with the Ministry of Agriculture on resistance to virus diseases in potatoes, Monsanto agreed to donate the coat protein events that confer virus resistance to PVX and PVY in potatoes and the Rockefeller foundation sponsored the three-year research. There are various ongoing projects which are looking at crops like papaya and where public institutes in African and Asian countries are main partners. It is in some of these countries where the technologies are most needed to management relevant crops where environmentally safe solutions are not available. It is vital that governments, public institutes and industry work together.

Today in most of Western European countries there still remains a strong opposition to biotech crops. Several countries still do not permitting their commercial production and impose a high cost for conducting field trials given the safety regulations in place. We can also add that even though governments are supporting research and the public institutes are doing a great job in communicating their findings to the general public, NGO's have established a strong media presence and a unique influence on citizens. It will be interesting to see how the current perception changes in the years to come.

Education and suitable technology transfer for sustainable growth

The success of being able to feed the growing population and at the same time produce sustainably will not be possible if people working in agriculture are not provided with the necessary knowledge as well as suitable technologies that can be properly implement in there environments. Today around one out of three people in the globe are employed in agriculture. It is in Sub-Sahara Africa, South and East Asia where the largest proportion of the population are employed in agriculture. Most of the people in these regions live in rural poor areas and the figures show that women constitute the major work force in agriculture. No doubt improving education and empowering women in these regions will contribute to increase productivity, alleviate poverty and create sustainability.

The smart and step-wise introduction of new technologies respecting the capabilities and needs of the farmers is imperative. What has been seen to be successful in an industrialized country might not be the case in a developing country, and might require adjustments. With the enormous choice of mechanical tools and crop varieties that have been developed in the industrialized countries we often see that farmers in China or India make interesting adjustments which best fit their needs in the field. Agronomic technology transfer is not only about understanding agronomical practices and economics; it is also having an appreciation and respect of the environment and the culture.

References

1 The International Fund for Agricultural Development (IFAD). Water Facts and Figures.
http://www.ifad.org/english/water/key.htm

2 Smithsonian Magazine (2011-01-05). "The Rise of Urban Farming". http://www.smithsonianmag.com/40th-anniversary/the-rise-of-urban-farming-762564/

3 Young, S.L., Meyer, G.E., Woldt, W.E. (2014) Future Directions for Automated Weed Management in Precision Agriculture. Published in Automation: The Future of Weed Control in Cropping Systems (Chapter 15), pp. 249-259

4 Wand, Z.L. (2007) Nanopiezotronics. Adv. Mater., 19, 889–892
http://www.nanoscience.gatech.edu/paper/2007/07_AM_5.pdf

5 GroNtech www.youtube.com/watch?v=Ui3xTzBBmaE

6 International Service for the Acquisition of Agri-Biotech Applications (ISAAA Brief 49-2014) Global Status of Commercialized Biotech/GM Crops:
2014 http://isaaa.org/resources/publications/briefs/49/executives ummary/default.asp

7 United States Department of Agriculture (USDA), Economic Research Service (ERS). 2014. Genetically Engineered Crops in the United States. Feb. www.ers.usda.gov/publications/err-ecomomic-research-report/err162.aspx

10

The Future of The Arts: Intermediality

GERMÁN GIL-CURIEL, PH.D.*

Research Affiliate in Music at University College Cork.

T he future of the arts is intermediality, that is, a trend to convergence. As a means of expression and exchange, the different media depend on and refer to each other, both explicitly and implicitly; they interact as elements of particular communicative strategies; and they are constituents of a wider cultural environment. The intermedia terminology has been employed to stress the innovative or transgressive potential of artworks that articulate their message in the interstices of two media forms. Previously the term Gesamtkunstwerk, attributed to Richard Wagner, had been used to describe an artwork that would reintegrate the theatre, music, and the visual arts of ancient Greek drama into Opera, and eventually, into cinema. Although the term 'Gesamtkunstwerk' accrued negative associations given Wagner's alleged connections with fascism, this idea of hybridity and mixing— intermediality—is nonetheless the future of the arts. Below, I provide some examples of this, and offer some concluding remarks.

Architectural Music

Apart from filmed musical performances, which involve a stage with all the traditional paraphernalia to create a captivating spectacle, the industry has diversified throughout time, in search of new auxiliary elements that can enhance the performance and present more spectacular shows. One instance of this has been the mixture of architecture and music, such as old magnificent buildings or churches, which also provide very good acoustics. From the *Bolivian Baroque* such as the missions of *Chiquitos* and *Moxos* Indians, which was filmed in the Church of Concepción in the middle of the Bolivian jungle, to *Jacques Loussier's Trio* playing Bach at St Thomas Church in Leipzig or Sting's concert *Winter's Night* at Durham Cathedral, music is more than simply heard in all these settings, actively interacting with them instead.

Furthermore, musical performances that are filmed live are increasingly incorporating other elaborate choreographies that include dance and fashion (as I discuss below), providing the performance with new spectacular dimensions. *Il Giardino Armonico* (The Garden of Harmony), an innovative project created by Luca Pianca and Giovanni Antonioni in Milan, centers around the baroque. The ensemble performs with virtuoso soloists. But the setting, music and dance all contribute to an intermedial *mise-en-scene*, allowing the show to convey a genuine atmosphere with a new concept of spectacle. In Japan, Kitaro Tamayura's music video of the same name 'features wildly colorful scenes and surreal, almost magical dance routines', also enabled by and enhanced with technology. Last is the case of, Tan Dun, the most celebrated Chinese pioneer composer of hybrid music, who draws from Eastern and Western traditions. Tan Dun's visual music, as the main protagonist of his multi-media installations, brings traditional ethnic music into dialogue with the latest technology, mirroring a process that is taking place in a wider scale all over China today (Gil Curiel, forthcoming). Tan Dun's visual music is all about hybridity: multimedia presentations involving nature, music, performance, dance, architecture, landscape and cinema, in which every medium provides a unique contribution. Tan Dun's work is truly innovative, mixing media and traditions, interweaving the visual with the auditive and even the performative in ways reminiscent of theories of total art.

Image 1. Intermedial Performance: nature as setting, architecture, and a screen that brings performers into co-presence with the musicians in a different time frame.

Cinematic Paintings

Another clear example of the intermedial future of the arts can be found in the work of Peter Greenaway, in particular his multimedia installations, which leads us to the realm of painting interacting with cinema, digital visual technology, music and literature. I am referring to the project 'Classical Paintings Revisited', which involves the re-creation of nine iconic Western art paintings by means of various media. *The Wedding at Cana* by Paolo Veronese is one of these paintings. The performance, set to soundtrack, consists of superimposing digital imagery and projections, such as close-up images of faces and diagrams onto the painting, showing interrelations and similarities between cinema and painting, in relation to the painter's mastery of perception, as 'cinema is nothing if it is not to be considered as the manipulation of light' (Greenaway p. 4). Also, music and dialogues for the 126 characters painted in Veronese's *Wedding at Cana*— wedding guests, servants, onlookers and wedding crashers—interact with the visual effects. Greenaway's project sets in motion a high-tech-mediated dialogue with the original paintings.

In like manner, the painting *Qingming Shang He Tu* ('Scenes along the River during the *Qingming* Festival'), a scroll more than five-meter panorama running from right to left, has been digitized, again bringing painting, music and cinema into the mixture. The painting is the monumental masterpiece by Zhang Zeduan (1085-1145), a court painter during the reign of Emperor Huizong of the Song Dynasty, considered to be one of the most renowned works in Chinese art history. It focuses on themes related to daily life, depicting the hustle and bustle of people during the celebration of the *Qingming Festival* in China. The animated digital version of the painting, occupying a full wall, was shown in the Shanghai World Expo in 2010 presented at the China Pavilion. It became an animated long mural about 30 times the size of the original scroll.

Fashion

Film and fashion have a long history of collaboration. The synergy between both industries enjoyed a symbiotic relation from the very beginning of the invention of cinema: the fashion industry has taken advantage of film as a means to enhance creativity and boost sales, and the film industry has also incorporated fashion for the same purposes. However, this collaboration has reached new heights with recourse to intermediality. The clearest example of this is perhaps the work of Scottish fashion designed Alexander McQueen (1969-2010). He has been one of the most influential, imaginative and provocative designers of postmodern times. His designs both questioned and expanded conventional practices of fashion to introduce new ideas regarding culture, politics and identity. The epitome of fashion, McQueen's creations go beyond marketing conventional clothing to explore fashion's ideological and conceptual possibilities, considering a broad range of components that make identity: social class, gender, sexuality, morality and religion.

McQueen's spectacles have had a great impact in the fashion industry for both the radical experimentation of his designs, often embodying a darker strain of Romanticism, and for the innovative ways in which he presented these, around a show whose concept was frequently inspired by cinema, but also drew from theatre, dance and music, and even the circus and other forms of spectacle. Let us quote, for instance, McQueen's *Deliverance* collection, which is composed of a complex network of inter-textualities that comprise literature, theatre, cinema, painting, music, dance and fashion. His show was inspired by Sydney Pollack's 1969 film, *They*

Shoot Horses, Don't They?, which in turn was an adaptation of Horace McCoy's homonymous novel written in 1935, the times of the Great Depression in the United States. The novel has inspired an intricate sequence of adaptations, from Pollack to McQueen. McQueen may well have seen some of these adaptations. At any rate, he re-creates the tragic dance marathon that is at the heart of the novel and the film for his collection's fashion show. This spectacular presentation took place in Paris in October 2003, in the Salle Wagram dance hall. Michael Clark choreographed the performance with the participation of models together with professional dancers. The key features that make Alexander McQueen's fashion spectacles so relevant to our times are precisely its tragic dimension and the way it draws from the narrative and the spectacle potential from the other arts—notably theatre, literature, film, music and dance—to create an integral artistic practice in fashion.

Image 2: Alexander McQueen recreates the marathon dance scenes from the film *They Shoot Horses, don't they?* (upper image) to present his fashion collection (lower image).

Conclusion

To conclude, the future of the arts lies in hybridity, not only with extensive cross-fertilization across and between the arts as such, but also between arts and industries, arts and technologies, and importantly, across cultures around the world.

References

Gil-Curiel, Germán. "Chinese Identity: Poetics of Cinema and Music in Hero." Film Music in 'Minor' Cinemas. Ed. Germán Gil-Curiel. New York: Bloomsbury, 2016. 71-89.

—. Dancing Tragedy: Alexander McQueen's Aesthetics of Spectacle. 2013. 17 10 2015 <http://fashion.semiotix.org/2013/02/dancing-tragedy-alexander-mcqueens-aesthetics-of-spectacle/>.

Greenaway, Peter. Paolo Varonese. The Wedding at Cana. Milan: Charta, 2010.

McCoy, Horace. They Shoot Horses, Don't They? London: Serpent's Tale, [1937] 2010.

They Shoot Horses, Don't They? Dir. Sidney Pollack. 1969.

11

Self-initiated expatriation and the importance of raising multicultural children

YESMITH SÁNCHEZ, M.SC.*

Strategy and communication coordinator at Kolibrí Festivaali, Finland.

When we choose our profession, in my case at seventeen years old, we don't always know where it may lead us. I chose Business Management because I figured it would be flexible enough, and it is, it is one of those degrees where you know a little bit of everything but your specialization will come with your career as you are shaping it in the working life. My Master's degree in International Management and Strategy was a decision that I made because I aimed to have further specialization on the field and when, in order to pursue my degree, I made research on self-initiated expatriation, I opened a world of opportunities, both on a professional and on a personal level that are currently relevant and of tangible use for myself and my host society.

As a professional with foreign background in Finland and as a mother of two, the topic of multiculturalism is highly relevant for me. What is the impact of our work and networks we build when it comes to raising children within a multicultural society?

In the light of the current migration crisis and when it is a topic that is in newspapers on a daily basis, a big part of political discourse and a situation that concerns all of us, citizens; it is important to define our role as individuals in a country different from our place of birth, how to contribute to our host society and how to impact future generations through knowledge sharing and bridging opportunities.

Self-initiated expatriation in Finland

Self-initiated expatriates are defined by Howe-Walsh and Schyns (2010:262) as "employees who decide to migrate to another country for work. Self-initiated expatriates initiate their expatriation and find a position in another country by themselves". Parting from this definition, a large majority of professional Mexicans living abroad fit into the so-called self-initiated expatriate (SIE) category.

According to the statistics (migri.fi, 2014) the number of non-Finnish nationals in Finland has been increasing steadily in the latest years but it has been increasing not only in numbers but also on diversity of motivations and backgrounds of the foreign population. According to the statistics, family ties is the largest motivation to move to Finland.

Finland, which has historically been considered an emigration rather than an immigration country (Akhlaq, 2005), in the recent years, has been having a greater immigration than its emigration, however, according the annual report on migration 2010, more highly skilled workers are moving abroad from Finland than to Finland, this means than in total, they are suffering a brain drain that is not compensated by the brain gain that highly qualified immigrants represent. Another characteristic of the migrant population in the country, is that the largest minorities continue to be from the neighboring countries (Estonia, Russia and Sweden) and nearly 65% of the foreign population concentrates in Helsinki and the metropolitan area (Sánchez, 2014). According to the annual report on immigration 2012, the unemployment rates among foreign nationals are far higher than the whole population rate being in average by the time when the report was published of 25.15% and 8.29% respectively.

According to the findings of my study, the main motivation for Latin American professionals to move to Finland is related to pursue further education which Carr et al. (2005) consider "career factors". The decision of coming to study in Finland is heavily affected by it being tuition free and to build an international career and in a lesser extent, some of the interviewees, used studies as a mean to later stay in the country. Another reason for moving to the country was related to a personal motivation, i.e. having a Finnish partner.

The study identifies the perceived barriers for integration in the host society not only on a personal level but also and particularly in the professional field and the main perceived barrier was a lack of command of Finnish language. Although the language is perceived as relevant for finding a job and for integration in daily life, it was pointed that it is a language that is difficult to learn, learning it is a long process and courses are not offered by the integration programs to those that have come to the country in order to achieve a degree. Other perceived barriers were the high difficulty of finding a job, the employers' skepticism and discrimination, bureaucracy and cultural differences.

The factors identified as facilitators for integration were having a job and building and using networks as social capital. Interestingly enough, when asked about the integration programs that the government offers and that are part of the reputable Finnish welfare, interviewees perceived that they did little in order to help them in their integration because of a perceived priority given to refugees over self-initiated expatriates.

Immigration in general continues to increase in Finland according to the statistics and self-initiated expatriation is part of this increase and researching the topic from an International Management perspective is relevant. Quoting Carr et al., (2005), "business operating internationally must often choose between local people, staff expatriated by the company, and immigrants. Understanding migrants is, therefore, of major importance in international management.". Taking this as a basis, the implications are tightly related to human resources management where recruiters, working teams and policy makers need to take into consideration this "new" multicultural arena in their decision-making.

Network building has been identified as crucial in Finland for integration of migrants as well as in the job-hunting process for both, foreign and Finnish nationals. If as concluded in my research, one of the main facilitators for integration is having a job and being able to actively participate in the host society, research on how to improve the quality of such networks for self-initiated expatriates is of high relevance.

Kolibrí Festivaali and multiculturalism

The festival Kolibrí is a way to experience multilingualism and multiculturalism through art expressions. We aim to promote the use of Spanish and Portuguese language for children that have been born in Finland or are living in the country and one of the parents has one of those languages as their mother tongue. The festival offers artistic and recreational activities for the whole family and brings a multidisciplinary program in a multicultural setting which is open to different kinds of families, irrespective of nationality or language.

Through these activities we hope to create awareness of the increasing multicultural population and to inspire other language and cultural minorities to also share their cultural heritage through art, research or open discussions in order to contribute in the building of a Finnish society that is more mature and open to its increasing heterogeneous society.

During the 2015 festival took place in spring and fall. Kolibrí not only offered open workshops to families of all backgrounds, but also organized discussion panels about the "new finns", their integration, prejudices, education and opportunities and a seminar about the role of the father in the acquisition of a language for their children when living in a country where the same is not spoken. This seminar aimed to offer information and proposals on how to enhance bilingualism in children and to create a platform for fathers who are trying to teach their children either Spanish or Portuguese when their spouse does not have the same mother tongue and is not the family language. This seminar was part of the cycle "Global

Helsinki" which was the topic for ThinkFest of the University of Helsinki.

Shaping the future

So what are the challenges for professionals dealing with multiculturalism and migration issues? What is going to be our contribution for future generations? How can we create a more open and multicultural society? These are the questions of no easy answer, nevertheless, starting the mental exercise of answering them may be already one step forward towards shaping a future where our children are going to deal with an even greater diversity than the one we are facing today. It is important to provide future generations with tools such as language and intercultural skills that will build cooperative societies and where differences can be capitalized into social, scientific and business solutions.

Changes in societies tend to be slow and it takes generations to actually perceive tangible changes, that is why, the contribution of multilingualism and multiculturalism is a long term project. Establishing short term goals is imperative in order to achieve the long term desired results, by 2050, some of our kids will be facing new challenges when trying to raise their children and while trying to keep their cultural heritage. Trying to visualize how that is going to be, is merely a fantasizing, but it is in our power and best interest to raise children that are culturally sensitive and that embrace differences.

Conclusion

The role of research in self-initiated expatriation as well as other forms of migration is crucial in today's world and particularly relevant in the midst of the current refugee crisis affecting mainly Europe. Assessing the role of various stakeholders in building a more open and multicultural society is a multidisciplinary task. Education of children, both in schools and within the family is probably going to play the biggest role in this imminent evolution, but we all have to ask how we, in our different fields, are affecting it.

From and International Management perspective, I continue to identify human resource management and optimization of talent as one of the areas of opportunity for managers, governments, universities and entrepreneurs. Knowledge transfer to our home countries will also be a topic where we will want to pay attention, in this way, we will optimize the professional development of individuals into something of bigger impact for the home and the host societies.

As a strategist in a festival where we aim to promote multiculturalism and multilingualism through art expressions, the challenge will be on having a deeper impact than that that sporadic events can have. We will need to focus on sharing a message of the importance of raising multicultural children and in doing it ourselves. Our generation has already experienced increased voluntary world mobility and that has enriched practices in different fields, let's enhance a further evolution for those generations to come.

References

Akhlaq, A (2005): Getting a job in Finland: The Social Networks of Immigrants from the Indian Subcontinent in the Helsinki Metropolitan Labour Market. University of Helsinki. Department of Sociology. Academic Dissertation. Helsinki University Printing House.

Carr, S.C., Inkson, K. and Thorn, K. (2005): From global careers to talent flow: Reinterpreting 'brain drain'. Journal of World Business 40: 386-398

Howe-Walsh, L. and Schyns, B. (2010): Self-initiated expatriation: implications for HRM. The International Journal of Human Resource Management, Vol. 21, No. 2: 260-273.

Kolibrí festivaali website, visited on October 18th, 2015. Available from URL: [http://www.kolibrifestivaali.org/en/about/]

Ministry of the interior. (2011): Annual report on immigration 2010. Available from URL: [http://www.migri.fi/download/16939_maahanmuuton_vuosikats aus_eng_netti_1_.pdf] consulted on April 15, 2014.

Ministry of the interior. (2013): Annual report on immigration 2012. Available from URL: [http://www.migri.fi/download/46518_46515_Maahanmuuton_til astokatsaus_2012_ENG_web.pdf?15f8588f92fbd088] consulted on April 15, 2014.

Sánchez, E. Y., (2014): Breaking the ice: An exploratory study on the factors that influence the integration of Latin American self-initiated expatriates in Finland.

The Finnish immigration service, consulted on March 17th, 2014, available from URL: [http://www.migri.fi/for_the_media/statistics]

12

Achieving human rights: a disability perspective

GENEVIEVE RUIZ-O'SULLIVAN*

*Social Researcher, Centre for Effective Services, Dublin, Ireland.

...more than a million people in the world today experience disability. People with disability have generally poorer health, lower education achievements, fewer economic opportunities and higher rates of poverty than people without disabilities.   -World Health Organization

Personally, through my journey as a professional working with and for people with disabilities, I understand and I am aware of the history and the progress made in the last 10 years in the disability sector. But this is a change that is taking place at a very slow pace and driven by people with disabilities themselves and their families. This article will focus on the future living conditions of people with disabilities. But before envisaging the future, it is crucial to look at the not faraway past, because perhaps the only way to generate an equal future for people with disabilities is to be aware of the past and not allow for the past to be repeated.

A glance into the past

Throughout history and around the world, individuals with a disability have been treated as lesser human beings. Numerous tags has been used with a connotation of inferiority: 'invalid' 'underdeveloped', 'crippled', 'lunatic', 'spastic' 'retarded' 'handicap' and the list goes on. The inequality experienced by disabled people has been characterized by how, historically, overlooked their opinions, civil rights and human rights have been. For instance, the construction of institutions for disabled people made evident the confiscation of their right of choice, specifically related to where and with whom to live.

Institutions[1] for people with disabilities originated as a humane response to the oppression and misery created by the new demands of increasing industrialized communities. As Kapp argues, institutions were often the preferred choice by many families who struggled with criticisms from society. In some countries, the introduction of mandatory schooling identified those who had difficulties in 'ordinary schools' giving place to categorization of "educable" and "uneducable". Those considered "educable" were provided with education, while the "uneducable" were allocated in institutions regardless of their age. Although institutions were originally created with the intention of protecting and providing adequate assistance for people with disabilities, soon the conditions in institutes deteriorated and residents experienced isolation and poor care conditions. Various types of institutions were established for adults and children with disabilities such as residential homes, boarding schools, lunatic asylums, residential homes and special hospitals. All of them were located in remote areas and soon the number of people accommodated in those institutions peaked all over Europe causing overcrowding and poor living conditions for residents.

Despite the implementation of new international and local legislation, the experiences in daily life of people with and without disability differ greatly. Research in the area of disability rights has focused on aspects that may reduce the inequality (e. g. living accommodation, education and employment).

People with disability exercising their rights

Although people with disabilities were protected by general human rights conventions, this did not stop the violation of many of their human rights. This was especially true for those with intellectual disability who were forgotten by movements working for the recognition of fundamental human rights.

Nowadays, a point of reference for policy makers and professionals working in the disability sector is certainly the United Nations Convention on the Rights of Persons with Disabilities (CRPD) as it is the first international treaty to specifically address the rights of disabled people. It is considered the most advanced and complete document available containing their rights. The Convention defines 'disable' individuals as "those who have long-term physical, mental, intellectual or sensory impairments which in interaction with various barriers may hinder their full and effective participation in society on equal basis with others" (United Nations, 2006, p. 5). Therefore, the Convention adopts the social model perspective of disability, where 'disability' is placed in the barriers that the environment and society impose, hindering their full inclusion in society; rather than on the persons' impairments.

The CRPD includes human rights contained in other human rights treaties. However, the Convention is set in principles that protect the equality, dignity, inclusion, independence and autonomy of people with disabilities. The Convention has been signed by 159 countries around the world and ratified by 151. It contains 50 Articles such as the right to live independently and being included in the community (article 19); the right to personal mobility (article 20); the right to work on an equal basis with others (article 27); the right to participate in cultural life (article 30) and the right to be free of exploitation and abuse (article 16). This article will specifically focus on the 'right to live independently and being included in the community' to provide a perspective on the possible future of living accommodation and social equality for this sector of the population.

Living independently and being included in the community as a human right issue

Countries around the world are moving towards de-institutionalization and community living. De-institutionalization is the practice of moving people (regardless of their ability - mental or physical) from institutions into community-based environments. However, the transition appears to be a big challenge, even for States which had ratified it. For instance, in Mexico Rosenthal, Jehn & Galvan undertook a research on the living conditions of people with mental health problems in some institutions and documented high levels of cruelty and neglect. Examples like this, urge the Mexican government to truly implement the CRPD and bring legislation together to make a change. Similarly, developed countries such as the UK, will need to adjust local policy in order to accomplish the exercise of the rights stipulated in the CRPD such as living independently.

Overall, existing literature in this area suggests that although the CRPD has the potential to make a real change in the lives of disabled people, a number of issues need to be addressed in order to move from policy to implementation. Ireland is one example of a country that before ratifying the convention (made legally binding) first sought to adjust local legislation to make it a reality.

The ratification and adjustment in local legislations will continue in years to come and it is an important development, but inherent to the success of the implementation will be the provision of adequate supports during the transition from institutions to independent living as it might leave disabled people without knowing how to cope with the change. As it was mentioned by Hans S. Reinders, a professor of Ethics, rights-based approaches "open doors but fail to change what happens when people walk through them". So foreseeing the future, the right to live independently and living in the community for people with disabilities will mean not only legislation but a network of supports in the community.

In many countries, institutions still persist. Sweden and Norway are the only two countries where the closing of all institutions has been achieved, thus those nations are considered leaders in the field.

Taking a closer look at the leading country in deinstitutionalization shows that about 1.5 million people in Sweden have a disability [2] of some kind. In regard to the housing of people with intellectual disability (ID), the majority live in *group housing* which are situated in regular neighborhoods and consist of a number of apartments with their own bedroom, living room, kitchen and bathroom with a range of shared areas and 24 hours assistance. Another option is *serviced apartments* where they can live independently with the option of calling for assistance when necessary. Regulations now exist that limit the maximum number of people living in a group home to five. Contrary to these regulations, in a recent inspection, it was reported that some accommodate up to 12 people. Similarly, researchers in the area (Tideman, Tossebro) argue that people with intellectual disability in Sweden are currently living under similar conditions to those in the 1990's because not much has been achieved in providing equal living standards for persons with and without ID. Among those gaps are the limited opportunities for participation and self-determination; the recurring practice of labelling individuals as 'intellectually disabled; variation between persons' living conditions subject to municipalities/areas in which they live and insufficient society-oriented disability research.

The series of problems detected in Sweden, have proved that despite the accomplishments, disparity still exists and this, without a doubt is disturbing as there is now a new term arising: *re-institutionalization*. A not very positive future then is already appearing on the horizon? The author believes that lessons learned from leading countries will be the key for the successful planning and implementation of deinstitutionalization.

Therefore, closing all institutions does not guarantee equal opportunities, better services and equal conditions.

More is required, especially adequate and effective disability policy. In a recent European study, it was reported that there were over a million people with disabilities living in residential institutes in Europe despite there has been a marked emphasis in supporting the de-institutionalization.

The United Nations and the European Commission called for a firm commitment to de-institutionalization underlying that the right to live in community setting is closely linked with fundamental rights such as personal liberty, private and family life, and freedom from ill-treatment or punishment (Council of Europe, 2012). Furthermore, the EU has established the "European Disability Strategy 2010-2020" with the intent that people with a disability in the EU enjoy their full rights and they are being included in society.

Social inclusion

The Article 19 in the CRPD refers also to social inclusion and a growing body of research has identified key factors on this: being accepted and recognized as an individual beyond the disability; being in contact with family, friends and other people; being involved in recreation, leisure and other social activities; having appropriate living accommodation, employment and adequate support. Many of these are underestimated and taken for granted by able-body persons, but it is not a reality for the majority of people with disabilities. For instance, in the case of individuals with mental health problems anti-stigma and antidiscrimination initiatives are also necessary to promote their inclusion.

Stigma and discrimination affects people's dignity, their civil, political, economic, social status, their cultural rights, thus limiting their opportunities. Discrimination adopts various forms, and so often discriminating behavior blends so subtly into the environment that nobody is able to recogni`e stigma and rejection towards people with disabilities. To achieve their social inclusion, it will be required more than legislation, it is critical a better awareness and understanding by society of the implications that labels and stereotypes have on adults and children with a disability.

A place, a home to live in

Shelter is considered one of the most basic human needs and this interlinks with living conditions such as choosing where and with whom to live. Isn't it wrong that a big proportion of people with disabilities do not have control over such matters? Most people will agree that a place to live (a place to call 'home') is not only about having a 'roof over the head' but about living conditions, living with dignity and having access to services in the community and being included in society.

To conclude, thousands of people with disabilities around the globe continue living in congregated settings. In those settings, people are compelled to live together and isolated from society. For the great majority of those people, their living conditions go against basic rights and against policies of social inclusion.

While the CRPD, together with reforms in education (early intervention for children with ID), technological innovation (cochlear implants, robotic limbs), and Universal Design (more accessible environment) may progress the achieving of equality in the decade ahead; it may not be sufficient. It is essential to be mindful of our history as a society, and taking a retrospective view may guide the necessary steps to take towards closing the breach between discrimination and inequity and accomplish a more equal future amongst humans.

---

[1] Institution, for this article, is defined as *"any place in which people who have been labelled as having a disability are isolated, segregated and/or compelled to live together. An institution is also any place in which people do not have, or are not allowed to exercise control over their lives and their day-to-day decisions. An institution is not defined merely by its size"* (European Coalition for Community Living, 2013). This definition broadens the usual concepts that focus on the physical size of a building or the number of people living there.

[2] Disability is defined in current Swedish legislation as: permanent physical, mental or intellectual limitation of a person's functional capacity that as a consequence of injury or illness existed at birth, has arisen since then or can be expected to arise (Swedish Discrimination Act, 2008).

13

Mexico City Airport Case: a Simulation-based Study

EDGAR MENDOZA DORANTES

MIGUEL MUJICA MOTA*

CATYA ZUNIGA ALCARAZ**

Researcher and lecturer at the Aviation Academy of the Amsterdam University of Applied Sciences in the Netherlands.

**Researcher, *Aeronautical University in Queretaro, Mexico*

One of the most important challenges for the aviation industry of this century is the continuous growth of air traffic. Diverse international institutions related with the aviation industry have elaborated forecasts about the behavior of the air traffic in the coming years. According to ICAO [1], in 2015 it is expected an increase of 6.3% in global passenger traffic. The global market forecast by Airbus [2], predicts an increase of the 6.6% annually for Latin America region (in terms of RPK3). Boeing states a similar forecast, with a 5.0% increase on the airline traffic per year (in terms of RPK) [3]. The National Chamber of Air Transport (CANAERO, by its acronym in Spanish) has estimated that in 2014 the flights market worldwide increase 4.7% annually meanwhile airlines in Latin America registered an increase of 5.9% [4].

Due to the imminent growth worldwide, it is very important to find some economic ways to propose effective solutions in the short, medium and long term, especially when the capacity of the airfield in major airports is reaching critical levels. In this sense, airfield capacity can be understood as the ability of a component of the airfield to accommodate aircraft, expressed in operations per unit of time. Although airport overall capacity is normally related to the runway system capacity, it can also be constrained by the ultimate capacity of other infrastructure elements such as runway system layout, apron area, or taxiway systems; the meteorological or environmental conditions; the demand characteristics; or even the business model of the airport, as well as their interrelation to each other [5, [6].

Hence, to overcome the increasing demand, it is helpful to analyze the capacity of other infrastructure elements related to airfield operations. Specially, the management of landing and departure flights to a specific gate is one of the key elements constraining the system which involves as key elements the runway and taxiway system. One way to analyze and find efficient solutions is by means of simulation models. Simulation is one the most popular techniques to plan airport operations because they provide realistic estimation by randomizing the various inputs parameters [7].

In this work, a discrete event system approach is used to study the main elements that constraint the capacity of the airside at Mexico City International Airport, i.e. runway and taxiway system and apron area in an integrated macroscopic approach. A preliminary model has been developed as a baseline to understand the current operation of the airport. The proposed simulation model incorporates the description of the airport operational environment and procedures to simulate air traffic movements. The operational environment consists mainly of airside facilities and associates operating procedures. Airside facilities include the runway, taxiway systems and apron areas. Operational procedures dictate runway use, taxi flows and gate allocation. Within this work, it is proposed a first approximation to the problem. Preliminary results have validated the approach and point out the benefits of it.

The structure of this study is described as follows: Section II describes the airfield components together with some important related works. Section III makes emphasis in the discrete event system approach as the technique; whereas section IV describes the modeling approach for the case study; section 5 analyzes the preliminary results obtained. Finally it is presented some conclusions about the case study.

Previous work

Typically, airport's facilities are divided into three components: airside, terminal, and landside. Airside facilities include elements that support the landing and takeoff operations, i.e. the transition of aircraft from air to ground and the movement of aircraft from parking (apron or storage areas) to runway. According to [8], the airfield itself is one component of the airside facilities, and typically encompasses the largest land area. Airside components include: maneuvering area (runways, taxiways, holding bays), aprons and gates. Airside support facilities include airfield maintenance, marking and lighting, navigational aids, weather reporting stations, and ATC facilities [2,5].

The maneuvering area can be understood as part of an airport to be used for the take-off, landing and taxiing of aircraft, excluding aprons. Apron(s) is defined by [9] as a defined area, intended to accommodate aircraft for purposes of loading or unloading passengers, mail or cargo, fueling, parking or maintenance. Aprons typically surround buildings, such as terminals and hangars, but also can be designed specifically to store aircraft out in the open using tied owns. A runway is defined as a rectangular area on a land aerodrome prepared for the landing and take-off of aircraft. Airports can have a single runway or multiple runways that may or may not be operated simultaneously [9]. The FAA [8] defines a taxiway as a paved strip of level ground along which aircraft taxi from the runway to a parking position (and vice versa) or from one part of the airport to another. Taxiways can also be used to temporarily hold aircraft waiting to take off or waiting for a gate. Gates within an airport are the access points between the aircraft and the terminal at which passengers typically embark or disembark. Gates may be at ground level or on an upper level, for which a loading bridge is provided to connect the aircraft to the door of the terminal building.

Diverse authors have tackled each of the elements of the airside to enhance capacity and other as integrated systems. These works can be classified respect to three main aspects: level of detail (macroscopic and microscopic), methodology (commonly analytical and simulation models), and coverage (a single element or integrated system).

Macroscopic approaches lead to approximate answers mainly for planning purposes and some design issues, with an emphasis on assessing the relative performance of a wide range of alternatives. These types of approaches allow a strategic perspective, which is crucial in the current context for the major airports around the world, especially when there is not enough financial resources for taking the decision of invest in the construction of more gates [10]. It can be found diverse literature that cover runway systems and gate allocation; there are very few models for taxiway systems or apron area.

There have been different approaches to enhance runway throughput. One of the first works dates from 1959 were it has been proposed an analytical probabilistic models for runway capacity estimation. Recently, a new perspective has risen from the air traffic management point of view. The landing sequence problem have been also studied to maximize runway throughput such as [11] based on Linear Programming which solves the static case presenting a mixed-integer zero-one formulation of the problem together with a population heuristic algorithm. A Dynamic-Programming-based approach which used a method called Constrained Position Shifting (CPS) as in [12]; In the work of [13], the merging and sequencing problems is addressed for a set of landing aircraft by genetic algorithms. It is aimed to minimize the number of conflicts encounter in landings while enhancing the runway feeding.

The gate assignment problem (GAP) has been studied from different approaches, but in general it aims to assign at every scheduled flight a gate, taking into account the total number of gates available in the airport, meanwhile keeping a balance between the time needed to receive the ground handling services, and the time for the next flight that it will be assigned at the same gate. The goal is to find an effective gate assignment for every scheduled flight using those scarce resources. It can be modeled in analogy to the NP-hard quadratic problem [14].

Tang and Wang [15] analyzed the GAP considering the airline's perspective in Taiwan Tao-Yuan Airport. In their approach, gate assignment is performed under airlines perspective rather than the airport authority. This study takes into account four components identified by the authors; the first two are related to the passenger service and the second ones with the operating efficiency. Through mathematical functions, they propose an objective function that seeks to maximize the combination of the four components. The results show that the third component, which seeks the maximization of the number of arriving flights assigned, and the subsequent departing flights assigned, to the same gate (if they are served by the same aircraft); dominates the other components and has a high importance in the gate assignment.

In the work of Diepen et al. [16], the gate assignment problem was analyzed with the case study of the Schiphol airport (Amsterdam). The main objective is to find a robust assignment of flights, presenting the problem as an integer linear programming with a cost function that assigns larger cost to schedules in which the probability of conflicts is higher. Through computational experiments, the authors found that with their method is possible to find practically optimal solutions for real-life instances in about 10 minutes, although they remark that the next step is to test the effect of optimizing their robustness objective in more detail and to analyze the quality of the solutions generated with the solutions presented by the software.

The departure metering is another approach to study the gate assignment problem. According to [17], this approach reduces taxi delays and emissions in the departure process while maintaining airport departure throughput. The authors used the traffic information of the LaGuardia airport (New York), through a queuing model intended to simulate potential queues on the airport surface. Thought the well-known tabu search technique, they solved the minimization the total overlap duration, which represents the major problem in the gate assignment that is known as gate conflict. The results show that the robust gate assignment helps airlines and air navigation service providers reap the benefits of departure metering because it leads to fewer disturbances to the gate assignment.

In the work of Narciso and Piera [10] it is remarked the important to study the behavior of the system, particularly the effect that delays could have in airport capacity. It is employed a causal modeling approach based on Petri nets formalism to analyze the system behavior. In their study, it is considered the effect of non-anticipated delay on gate occupancy. Their approach tackles the effect that delayed flights will have on the initial assignment of aircraft to gates at an airport, to design a robust gate assignment policy that mitigates arrival and turnaround delay effects while maximizing gate usability. The new policy takes into account the possibility to set up the total gates following four strategies: sequential assignment, distributed assignment, non-preemptive, and preemptive.

Discrete Event System

There is a large literature in the Discrete Event System (DES) field such as in [18], [19] or [20]. In this section, the concept of Discrete Event System (DES) will be introduced in order to understand the main approach used in this study. In that sense, the first key concept is system. According to Banks [18] a system can be defined as a group of objects that are joined together in some regular interaction or interdependence toward the accomplishment of some purpose. Weiner [21] defines a system as a natural or artificial entity, real or abstract, that is part of a given reality constrained by an environment. Another important author that has defined the system concept is Ackoff [22], which established that a system is more than the sum of its parts; it is an indivisible whole. It loses its essential properties when it is taken apart. The elements of a system may themselves be systems, and every system may be part of a larger system. Every system includes other systems (called sub-systems), but at the same time the whole system is a part of a superior system (supra-system). Because of that, the interaction and interrelation between each component of a system is fundamental to understand the whole system [19].

The contribution of Churchman [23] to the System Approach is to understand the vital importance of every part in a system, and the way in how they are interrelated (System Thinking). In addition, this author argues that the best way to understand a system is to define its role and purpose, and not by its structure. According to Gopal [24], a system implies two concepts: (1) interaction within a set of given or chosen entities, and (2) a boundary (real or imaginary), separating the entities inside the system from its outside entities. For that reason, when the goal is the analysis of a real life system, it is critical to have in mind, the natural constraints on the environment which make infeasible the experimentation with the real system. These constraints could imply the lack of sufficient resources like time, staff, expertise, or money; even it could be possible that the system does exist yet.

The components of a system are: entity, attributes, and activities. The entity is an object or component in the system which requires explicit representation in the model. An entity can be dynamic in that it "moves" through the system, or it can be static in that it serves other entities; the attributes are properties of that entity; whereas an activity represents a time period of specified length. Other important concepts within system theory are called the states and events. A state is the collection of variables necessary to describe the system at any time, relative to the objectives of the study; these variables are called state variables; while an event is an instantaneous occurrence that may change the state of the system [18].

Following the above definition, it is clear that most real life problems have too many interactions some hidden, some not, but then the question is-How to analyze a real life system if there are many interactions on it? It has been stated that humans have found different ways of dealing with these issues. One of them is to abstract the most important characteristics from the problem itself and then reason about it using a model of that problem. Then, a model can be defined as a representation of a system, and also as a simplification of the real system [18].

According to Weiner [21], systems can be classified depending on how the states variables and time are represented in the model as continuous and discrete. According to time base, there are continuous time paradigms, where time evolves continuously, and discrete time paradigms, where time evolves by advancing in discrete portions. On the other hand, if the values of the state variables are considered, there are continuous models, where the variables take their values from continuous set represented as a real number, and discrete models, where the variables are discrete and can be represented as a finite set of integer numbers.

It is possible to imitate a real-world problem through simulation, which means the imitation of the reality. Flores et al. [25] define the simulation as a numerical technique for producing experiments in a digital computer, using graphics, animation and others technological devices; which involve some mathematic and logical models, which describe the behavior of a system. Simulation involves the possibility to explore new policies and procedures without disrupting ongoing operations of the real system; also new systems can be tested without committing resources for their acquisition. In that sense, the time (an important resource) can be compressed or expanded with the simulation. Also the hypothesis of the researching can be tested for feasibility; and insight can be obtained about the interaction of variables. A simulation study can help in understanding how the system operates rather than how individuals think the system operates. In brief, the simulation can answer the question What if? This is useful in the design of new systems.

Mexico City Airport Case Study

Mexico City International Airport (MMMX4) is the principal airport in Mexico; its traffic has had a continuous growth since the recovery of the 2008 world economic crisis. In 2012, over 56.8 million passengers were transported through 618 regular routes, 355 international and 263 domestic. Passenger traffic has been forecasting to increase around 4.6% annually (in RPK) [26]. On this matter, it is substantial to point out that at the moment; the 34% of the total passengers transported in Mexico together with the 23% of the total number of operations in the country are concentrated in Mexico City International Airport [27].

During 2014, Mexico City International Airport experienced a tremendous growth on passenger traffic and the total number of operations. In fact, at the end of the year, the airport overcame its maximum capacity with a total of 34.2 million passengers (+ 8.6% in comparison with 2013), that means 2.4 million passengers over the available capacity [28]. Mexican authorities had established and declared a maximum capacity of 61 operations per hour with a total of 16 rush hours (7:00-22:59) [29]. In addition, during the saturated periods, the maximum operations had been exceeded in more than 52 times. The most congested periods are between 8:00-9:00hrs and 10:00-11:00 hrs. Furthermore, according to Herrera [30] during the last trimester of 2015 Mexico City Airport would reach 80% of its total capacity, which means a technical limit for being operable.

In this context, Mexican authorities announced in 2014, the construction of a new airport that will support the air traffic growth. Nevertheless, it is necessary to find alternative solutions while the current facilities are operating, especially if the construction of the new airport has been estimated to take between 6 to 10 years [27]. It is worth to remember that in more than 60 years of operations of Mexico City International Airport, 4 projects have been performed to deal with the traffic growth by expanding and remodeling different infrastructure, both in the land and airside.

The last project presented was in 2001, when Mexican authorities announced the constructions of a new airport to face the increase of air traffic, however this project was not implemented, due to some political and social tensions. Finally, within the same facilities, a second terminal building (T2)was built to alleviate traffic congestion. Nonetheless, it was clear that the facilities will not be enough to meet the demand of air traffic in a short-term period.

Despite the last announcement for building of new facilities, the current ones have to be analyzed in order to cope with the upcoming traffic demand. Therefore, it is needed to revisit some key elements in the system to be able to formulate strategic plans based on the performance of the overall system.

Table I. Airport characteristics

	Terminal 1	Terminal 2
Surface area	548 000 m^2	242 000 m^2
Contact positions	33	23
Remote positions	11	7+10
Other positions	9	2
Baggage carousel	22	15
Airlines	20	6

Mexico City International Airport has two passenger terminals called terminal 1 (T1) and terminal 2 (T2), interconnected by an internal train services and road access. The total surface area of the airport accounts for 756 ha. The airport is served by 26 passenger airlines and 17 cargo carriers [31]. See Table I for detail information.

The airport serves as the hub for Aeromexico (Mexican biggest airline), and, as the airline conforms the SkyTeam alliance, the airport has also become a SkyTeam hub.

Terminal 1 is mainly use for both national and international flights and it has a total of 44 gate/stand positons, 33 of them are contact gates (P1-P36) and 11 remote ones (S3-S8; P37-P40), as depicted in Fig.1. Terminal 2 is mainly use by international flights; it has 23 contact positions (G52-G74) and 17 remote ones (G75-G81) and (T1-T9; TA-TB) and a further area with 6 more positions (P48-P51; TC). There are also 7 customs clearance positions (P41-P47) in terminal 1. A total 107 gates are used at the airport; 56 are T1 and 51 in T2.

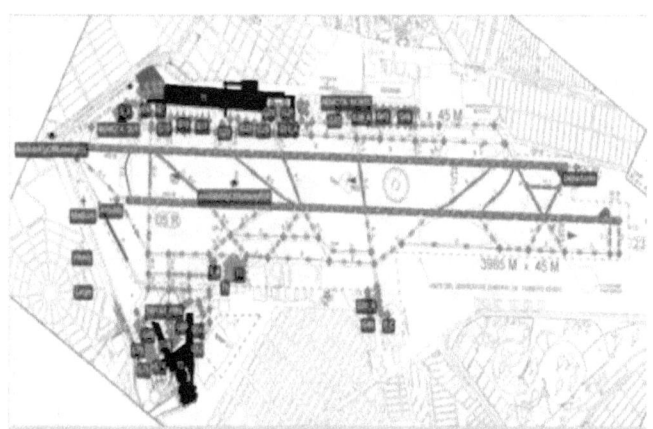

Figure 1.   Macroscopic view of the model

The runway system consists on runway 05L/23R and 23R/05L with dimensions 3963x45m and 3985x45m, respectively. The declared separation between them is 1000 ft. (305 m). According to FAA [8], independent operations (landings and/or departures) need 3000-4300ft (914-1311m) separations between runways which constraints independent operations; therefore, it is operated as a single runway. In current operations, one runway is used for arrivals and the other one for departures.

Nowadays, in the airport, the gate assignment is performed according with the airline perspective, which means that some gates are exclusives for one airline. Depending on the availability, the airport authority assigns for every scheduled flight a gate where the airline operates in the terminal buildings.

Table II. Runway bearing characteristics

Runway bearing	Gate
A: 23 M ASPH PCN 85/F/B/X/T	Departing from T2
A2: 23 M ASPH PCN 80/F/C/X/T	Departing from T1
A4: 25 M ASPH PCN 120/F/C/X/T	Gates 58-68
B: 23 M ASPH PCN 100/F/C/X/T	Approaching to T1
B3: 23 M ASPH PCN 73/F/C/X/T	Gates 69-81
C: 23 M ASPH PCN 100/F/C/X/T	Gates 37-47
D: 23 M ASPH PCN 100/F/C/X/T	Approaching to T2
E: 23 M ASPH PCN 120/F/C/X/T	Approaching to T2
E2: 23 M ASPH PCN 75/F/C/X/T	Gates 48-51
F: 23 M ASPH PCN 100/F/C/X/T	To release runway 23L/05 R
G: 23 M ASPH PCN 100/F/C/X/T	To release runway 23L/05R
J: 25 M ASPH PCN 120/F/C/X/T	Gates 56-57
PH: 25 M ASPH PCN 120/F/A/X/T	Gates 52-55 & TA,TB

The taxiway system has 19 runway bearing, Table II present the ones used within this work to model the taxiway. According to the airport policies an aircraft approaching to T1 exits runway by runway bearing F. In case the gate has been assigned form 1 to 36 then it is used runway bearing B to approach; it is used runway bearing C to arrive to north remote platform and customs clearance area. Aircraft assigned to T2 leave across runway bearing G. Once in the taxiway system, aircraft move on runway bearing E and D depending on the final destination of the aircraft. Aircraft use runway bearing E2 to approach to gates 48 to 51; runway bearing PH to approach to gates 52 to 55 and Tango remote; runway bearing J is cross to arrive to gates 56 to 57; runway bearing A4 is used when gates 58 to 68 are assigned; runway bearing B3 for gates 69 to 81; and finally runway bearing A and A2 are used for departing from T1 and T2, respectively.

The preliminary model to analyze Mexico City International Airport airside capacity at a macroscopic level is depicted in Fig. 1. The system is integrated by the runway system, taxiways, apron area and gates. Each of these elements has been modeled under an object orientated paradigm. The simulation has been developed using the SIMIO software through the use of historical data. Operational procedures information was quite difficult to obtain due to the lack of public information, the one used within this work was obtained from [30], [32], [33] and [34].

The model logic is described in Fig. 2. The process begin with the arrival of the scheduled flights, each flight has been classified according with the FAA [35] as: Heavy, Large and Medium. Before allowing a landing/departure operation, the controller needs to verify the availability of the runway. It is worthy to remember that in our case study, the use of runways is not simultaneously. Once runway is clear, each aircraft is allowed to take its taxiway route sequence and speed to its assigned gate. As soon as the aircraft enters the taxiway system, both runways are released for another incoming/departure flight. It has to be also verified if the taxiway is clear; if it is, then controller allows aircraft moves within it; in the opposite case, the flight waits until the taxiway is clear.

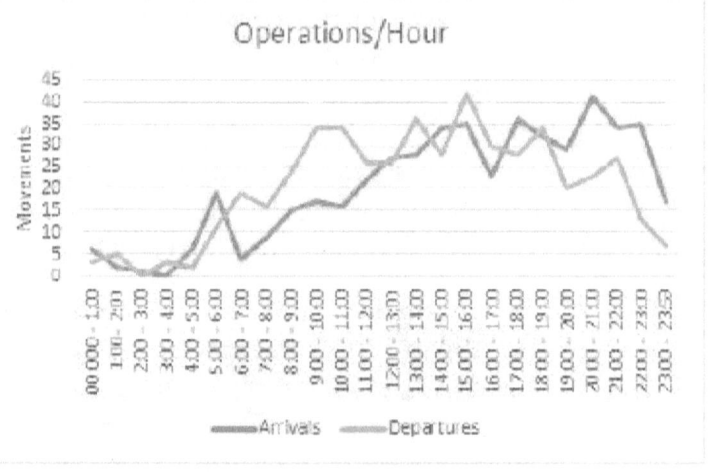

Figure 3. Demand example in a 24 hour

Figure 2. Process logic.

The handling operations are modeled by a time is consumed by the aircraft; each type of aircraft has been assigned with a different handling time in accordance of [30]. Once handling operations have finished, a depart sequence is assigned. The aircraft verifies again if the taxiway is clear, and when it is, aircraft is allowed to depart from its gate to runway 05L/23R. When aircraft reaches the runway bearing A or A2, it is verified against the availability of runways, if cleared, it starts its departing. The runway is release until the flight takes-off and leaves the final approach point. The process is iterative   for   all   daily   operations.

Table III. Handling time distributions

Distribution	Aircraft Type
Interval between 00:00 and 6:00 hours	
Johnson SB (0.7382, 0.4198, 0.9089, 68.63)	For the three classes
Interval between 6:00 and 23:59 hours	
Weibull (0.8675, 46.16)	A319
Johnson SB (1.525, 0.7471, 0.0132, 101.8)	A 320
Weibull (1.100, 23.89)	ATR
Beta (0.5861, 1.198)	B737
Johnson SB (0.7382, 0.4198, 0.9089, 68.63)	For heavy class
Pearson VI (1.065, 4.835, 209.4)	For large class
Pearson VI (1.129, 2.721, 129.2)	For medium class

Fig. 3 depicts the real demand distribution over a 24 hour period. It can be pointed out that between 20:00-21:00hrs, it is performed highest amount of arrivals operations, meanwhile departures have its peak between 15:00-16:00hrs with more than 40 operations. The scenario presented in this Fig. 3 corresponds to February 1st, 2015 with a total of 976 movements (arrivals and departures), which in turn represents a medium season day. Each arrival flight has attached information about the arrivals such as: estimated time of arrivals, aircraft type, gate assigned, arrival sequence, and handling time.

Handling time was considered through the application of four probability distributions: Jonson SB, Weibull, Pearson T6, and Beta. Those distributions were extracted from the work of Herrera [30]; they are related to aircraft type and obtained from the airport authorities, see Table III

Results analysis

After several experiments with the simulation model, the results show that the runway system is being utilized in an average of 54.23% of its total capacity, which suggests that it could be possible to increase the number of daily operations, especially between 0:00 and 6:00 hours, which is the lowest demand period. During that period there were registered 58 operations (arrivals and departures), which represents the 5.9% of the total operations of the February 1st, 2015.

As mentioned in the precious section, the gate assignment at Mexico City International Airport is performed base on the airline's perspective, i.e. certain gates are used only for some specific airlines. In this regard, it is important to remark that Aeromexico, has the biggest number of gates assigned in T2 due to its role as major airline in the country.

Table IV. Gates less used (time starved).

South Pier		North Pier		Remote Terminal 2	
Gate	Time Starved (min)	Gate	Time Starved (min)	Gate	Time Starved (min)
63	204	52	216	75	309
64	238	53	177	76	243
65	256	54	155	77	436
66	187	55	450	78	185
67	209	56	281	79	327
68	279	57	325	80	185
69	172	58	189	81	262
70	166	59	168		
71	159	60	164		
72	156	61	180		
73	236	62	201		
74	178				

The analysis also suggests that the capacity of the north and south piers in T2 could be increased, because both zones are used at the 18% of its total capacity. The table IV shows the time starved for every gate in each zone. The gates 52-81 at T2, are the gates with more time starved. The gates 75-81 have an average time starved of 278 min, while the gates 63-74 have a mean of time starved of 227 minutes. Gates 55, 56, 77, 79, and P75, are the one with highest time starved; which means that it could be possible to increase the utilization of these resources, at the same time than the capacity of the airport also increased.

Regarding the utilization of each terminal, T2 is the busiest one during the period analyzed with 13% of utilization in contrast to the 9.3% of T1. Each percentage was calculated by the sum of the mean utilization of every gate in T1 and T2, respectively. Fig. 4 shows the utilization of the gates according to the terminal where they are located. It is important to point out that, in spite of T2 is the busiest terminal; the number of gates with less occupancy time (time starved) is bigger than in T1. On the other hand, it is also important to note the average holding time or delay of a flight for landing is around 18.61 min which corresponds to the delay applied by the controllers before landing while the idle time of the both runways (measured as a single runway) is 4.78 min.

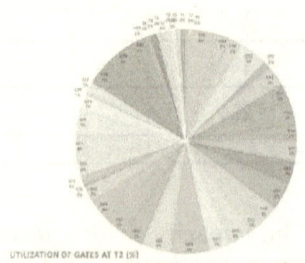

UTILIZATION OF GATES AT T2 (%)   UTILIZATION OF GATES AT T1 (%)

Figure 4.   Gate utilization per terminal

Table V. Operations during 2014

Month	Movements	%Change
Jan	32,768	-
Feb	29,939	9,449213
Mar	33,657	12,41858
Apr	33,734	0,228779
May	35,060	3,930752
Jun	32,945	6,032516
Jul	35,972	9,188041
Aug	36,071	0,275214
Sep	33,276	7,748607
Oct	35,761	7,467845
Nov	34,597	3,254943
Dec	36,174	4,558199
Mean %Change		5,9

Based on the above, five scenarios were designed in order to increment the traffic within the system and analyze it is possible performance under this assumptions. The goal is to use the previous information and to introduce in the system, some hypothetical flights called "dummy flights" in those areas that have been register with lower utilization and hence, to assign more flights to gate. The scenarios were designed according with the mean of the monthly percentage change of the operations during 2014, see table V.

Table VI summarized each designed scenario together with some important information. As depicted in table VI, 29 dummy flights were introduced in the first scenario (S1), 3which sum a total of 517 flights. The total number of operations in this scenario is 1033 operations per day. In that case, the runway system presents a utilization of 54.57%, the average delay applied before landing was 16.48 min, and the idle time was 4.63 min. This experiment, suggests that it is possible to increase the capacity of the runway system and decrease the idle time of the whole system.

In the case of the second scenario, 30 flights are introduced in the system, 1 flight more than in the first scenario, and significant differences were found. The main one is the delay introduced, since it increases to 35.6 min, while the idle time of the runway system decreases to 4.51 min. In this case, both runways are used at an average of 54.52%. On the other hand, it should be pointed out that for the third scenario, even 3 more flights were introduced (comparing with the first scenario) the utilization of runways is quite similar, with 54.51% but the delay introduced decreases compared to the one found in the second scenario, with an average of 16.90 min. Therefore, it has also been analyzed the behavior of the system based on the demand distribution over the day. Even more flights were introduced, these flights were added in the interval between 00:00 and 6:00 hours, and hence, the total delay introduced was quite similar to the first one. Then, not only on the number of flights added to the system affects the delay introduced, but their distribution per time slot.

Table VI. Scenarios

Scenarios	Dummy Flights	Number of Flights	Total Ops	Delay before landing	Idle Time
S1	29	517	1033	16.48	4.63
S2	30	518	1037	35.6	4.51
S3	32	520	1040	16.90	4.65
S4	125	613	1226	43.21	4.68
S5	161	649	1298	45.64	4.51

In the fourth and fifth scenario, the traffic increases significantly, with a total of 1226 and 1298 operations, respectively. The results note that the capacity of the runways system is used 54.59% and 54.4%, while the idle time increases to 4.68 and 4.51 min, for the fourth and fifth scenario respectively. As in the previous scenarios, flights were introduced in two different intervals. In the fourth scenario, the flights were added in the interval between 6:00 and 23:59 hrs meanwhile in the fifth scenario, flights were added in the interval between 00:00 and 6:00 hrs.

Conclusion

To overcome the growing demand at airports, a revisit of different activities is needed. The current situation of Mexico City International Airport is more delicate, mainly because it has been declared saturated in different slots by Mexican authorities. This and other forecasts have raised the need of a new airport which was announced last year. But until this project finishes, it will be necessary to enhance the capacity of different areas in the airport to cope with the increasing demand. This study focused in the airside encompassing the runways, taxiway and apron area as being the most restrictive systems within the airport.

A preliminary model was developed to analyze the behavior of the real system and to be able to predict different upcoming scenarios. Five scenarios were developed, in each one, the daily traffic was increased. Three critical key performance indicators were analyzed: the percentage of utilization of runways; idle time the runway system; and the delay introduced by controllers before landing.

The result demonstrates that if the air traffic demand rises, daily operations will suffer delays up to 45 min, and the congestion problem at the airport could become worst. The consequences of the increment in daily operations will not only affects arrivals but the other subsystems such as taxi system, gate assignment and handling operations among others.

There is plenty of future work within this approach. First, the model has to introduce more operational restrictions, which unfortunately, are not easy to identify, mainly due to the lack of public information of the airport. Detail procedures for taxiway should be introduced together with other gate assignment policies. Ground handling services should be modeled in detail to obtain a more accurate model. And other sample data, low and high season, for example, should be employed.

References

[1] ICAO (2013). Medium-Term Passenger and Freight Traffic Forecasts: World Air Transport in 2013, International Civil Aviation organization [website]. Retrieved from http://www.icao.int/sustainability/pages/eap_fp_forecastmed.asp x

[2] LEHAVY J. (2014), Flying on demand. Global market forecast, Airbus. Retrieved from http://www.airbus.com/company/market/forecast/

[3] BOEING (2014). Long-Term Forecast, Current Market Outlook 2014-2033. The Boeing Company [website]. Retrieved from http://www.boeing.com/boeing/commercial/cmo/

[4] CANAERO, (2014, August 24th). Monthly bulletin, National Chamber of Air- México [website], retrieved from http://www.canaero.org.mx/canaero/images/biblioteca/categorias /Boletin%20Agosto%202014.pdf

[5] NEUFVILLE R., ODONI A., (2003), Airport Systems: Planning, Design, and Management, McGraw Hill, United States.

[6] JANIC, M. (2008), Modelling the Capacity of Closely-spaced Parallel Runways using innovative approach procedures, Transportation Research Part C, 16704-730. doi:10.1016/j.trc.2008.01.003

[7]PENG Y., WEI G., JUNQING S. & BIN S. (2014), Evaluation of Airport Capacity through Agent Based Simulation, International Journal of Grid Distribution Computing Vol.7, No.6, pp.165-174.

[8] FAA, 2014. Aeronautical Information: Manual Official Guide to Basic Flight Information and ATC Procedures, Federal Aviation Administration, Washington, D.C., USA.

[9] ICAO, DEFINITION APRONS AND RUNWAY.

[10] NARCISO, M.E., PIERA, M.A., (2014). Robust gate assignment procedures from an airport management perspective, Elsevier Ltd.

[11] Beasley, M. Krishnamoorthy, Y. M. Sharaiha, and D. Abramson. Scheduling aircraft landings - the static case, 1998.

[12] H. Balakrishnan and Bala G. Chandran. Algorithms for scheduling runway operations under constrained position shifting. Oper. Res., 58:1650–1665, November 2010.

[13] Zuniga, C.A.; Delahaye, D.; Piera, M. A., 2011 Integrating and sequencing flows in terminal maneuvering area by evolutionary

algorithms, Digital Avionics Systems Conference (DASC), 2011 IEEE/AIAA 30th, vol. 2, no., pp.1-11S, 16-20 Oct. 2011

[14] CELA, E., (1998). The quadractic assignment problema: theory and algorithms, Kluwer: Dordrecht, US.

[15] TANG, C., WANG, W., (2013), Airport gate assignments for airline-specific gates, journal of Air Transport Management 30, 10-16.

[16] DIEPEN, G., VAN DEN AKKER, J.M., HOOGEVEEN, J.A., SMELTINK, J.W., (2012). Finding a robust assignment of flights to gates at Amsterdam Airport Schiphol, Springer Science Business Media, New York.

[17] KIM, S.H., FERON, E., (2014). Impact of gate assignment on Departure Metering, IEEE Transactions on Intelligent Transportation Systems, Vol. 15, No. 2, April 2014.

[18] BANKS, J., CARSON, J.S., NELSON, B.L., NICOL, D.M., (2010), Discreet Event System Simulation, 5th Edition, Pretince Hall, United States.

[19] BERTALANFFY, L. (1972), The History and Status of General System Theory, Center for Theoretical Biology, State University of New York at Buffalo, Academy of Management Journal.

[20] Cassandras, G.C. Lafortune S., Introduction to discrete event systems. Springer, 2009. 762 pages.

[21] WEINER, G.A., (2009), Modeling and Simulation: A practitioner approach, CR Press, United States.

[22] KIRBY, M., & ROSENHEAD, J. (2010), 'IFORS' Operational Research Hall of Fame', International Transactions In Operational Research, 17, 1, pp. 145-151, Business Source Complete, EBSCOhost, viewed 17 March 2015.

[23] CHURCHMAN, C. W. (1973). The System Approach, Diana, Mexico.

[24] GOPAL, M. (1993), Modern Control System Theory, 2nd Edition, New Age International Publishers, New Delhi, India.

[25] FLORES, I., FIGUERAS J., GUASCH A., MUJICA, M., NARCISO, M., PIERA, M. (2013), Simulation Models: Using Simio and Preti Nets, Universidad Nacional Autonoma de Mexico, Mexico.

[26] ROSA, A. (2014, September 1st). The AICM is in the limit of its operations. Forbes- Mexico. Retrieved from http://www.forbes.com.mx/aicm-en-el-limite-de-sus-operaciones/

[27] GOB (2014, April 28th), National Plan of Infrastructure 2014-2018. Mexican Government [online]. Retrieved from http://cdn.presidencia.gob.mx/pni/programa-nacional-de-infraestructura-2014-2018.pdf?v=1

[28] T21 (2015, January 28th). AICM overcame its maximum capacity during 2014, Magazine T21Mx [online]. Retrieved from http://t21.com.mx/aereo/2015/01/26/aicm-supero-su-capacidad-maxima-2014

[29] DOF (2014, September 29). Declaratory: saturation at the Mexico City International Airport. Official Newspaper of the Federation (DOF), Mexico.

[30] HERRERA GARCÍA A. (2012), Simulation Model of Airport Operation at Airports Congested, The case of Mexico City Airport, IMT, Technic publication No. 365, Qro., Mexico.

[31] AICM (2015). About the AICM, SCT. Retrieved from: http://www.aicm.com.mx/en/aicm_en/about-aicm/brief-history

[32] Flightstats Inc. (2015). Web page: http://www.flightstats.com/go/Home/home.do

[33] http://www.flightradar24.com/19.43,-99.07/14

[34] Aeropuertos y Servicios Auxiliares (ASA). Libro Blanco, Programa de Atencion a la Demanda de Servicios Aeroportuarios en el Centro del País [On line]. ASA: Coordinacion de las Unidades de Negocios, s.f. Retrieved from http://www2.asa.gob.mx/ServletRepositorio?id=95

[35] FAA (2013). Weight Class, Federal Aviation Administration (web). Retrieved from http://aspmhelp.faa.gov/index.php/Weight_Class

14

Mexican Diaspora 2025: the network that built bridges to nurture Mexico

JORGE ZAVALA, M.SC.*

*Founder, Red Global MX, Chief Disruptive Officer, Kinnevo

Mexico is a country with a mixed environment; from one side we came from a large immigration from Spain in the 15th century, our history as a country shows that we received foreign people both continuously and through some specific times like during the Spanish Civil War, during the 1973 Coup in Chile and during other events when Latin-American countries underwent economical or political problems.

From History to the Future

Recently, Mexico is becoming more attractive for immigration as stated by Pablo Magluf [1], but anyway Mexico has little immigration of foreign people coming to Mexico compared with the amount of people that leave Mexico to live abroad as is described in "La Migración Altamente Calificada: Elementos para una Política Nacional de Ciencia y Tecnología", by Raúl Delgado, et al. In the last 15 years, the profile of people leaving Mexico is changing drastically, before 2000 the low income people moved away mainly to the USA, recently people with higher education degrees are moving out of the country to have the experiences and opportunities that are available anywhere.

The Mexican Global Network (MGN) was born in 2005 as a concept and started its first chapter in Silicon Valley where the amount of highly qualified professionals came from students that came to the USA to pursue their master and PhD degrees, or executives from very large companies that had a subsidiary in Mexico and were transferred to the USA, this group was the first people that I discovered to ask for help to learn how Silicon Valley worked and got related to do business in the USA. From this initial experience, the MGN become at that time a way to build bridges between two different business cultures; on one side the Mexicans and on the other side the global mindset and innovation of Silicon Valley.

The creation of these bridges was an integrated work of business people based in Mexico looking for ways to reach global markets with the support of the Mexican government provided by the Minister of Economy, CONACYT and glued by the Minister of Foreign affairs connecting with the Mexican people living in Silicon Valley. These connections delivered a lot of conversations that enable new business opportunities, academic exchange, travels for explorations and recognition of new way of doing any kind of activities.

From the first chapter, locations like Boston, Washington, Houston and El Paso started their own chapters opening a communication channel from people in the USA and people in Mexico. Every year, from 2005 to 2012[2] every year the Instituto de los Mexicanos en el Exterior (IME) provided the support to bring the leaders in each chapter to hold a meeting in Mexico to foster the relationship of the Mexicans in both side of the borders with the people in government, academy and industry. These 7 meetings provided the grounds to establish networking among Mexicans living anywhere in the world and learn best practices of how business, academic activities and government relations are carried out in the new home of these group of Mexicans.

Then a great change was proposed to find the way to get together a large group of people and expand the reaching of the Mexican people around the world, in 2012 we have some fuzzy information about how many highly qualified people where living abroad, a number that was expected around 900,000 people. Therefore, each chapter had to expand their reach, find new ways or organizing and foster the development of new chapters around the world. In 2013, the IME help us to carried out the next global meeting in Chicago, where 22 chapters got together, a new support structure was proposed to foster the regional development in Europe, Asia and America.

The next two years brought the interest to more Mexican living abroad to reach in 2015 to have 45 chapters that allow to carried regional meetings and develop a much clear understanding of the role of the Mexican Global Network.

Each region has their own flavor and uniqueness, therefore in order to allow each chapter to fulfill their maximum potential a network of networks was the best way to allow freedom at the same time that provide value each node to each node. 2015 became to be the year where the delivery of this model provide an explosive growth of the MGN, more chapters where created around the world and bridges from any city in the world started to be built with every city in Mexico, the connection of chapters to nodes did a great bust to the organization. Each link, known as bridge, that connect a chapter with a node develops their own style, created their own agenda and facilitates projects around entrepreneurship, creative arts and science and technology.

From 2015 to 2025, the number of chapters and nodes grew to 1,345 with an exponential numbers of bridges; the MGN became the largest organized diaspora in the world that provided access to networks, knowledge, experience and resources from more than 5 million Mexicans living abroad. Looking how, the Mexican abroad became a strong and valuable resource that took 20 years to understand and developed has been one of the most complex processes that any one in the social sciences can imagine, we can see in their future a lot of research and publications that will uncover the secrets of an effort that thousand of anonymous heroes built without documenting. Thanks to the social networks and the technology available this effort will be feasible to the modern anthropologist to rebuilt the history and provide better grounds to keep developing the MGN model.

The flavor of Mexico

Mexico in the 20th century was a country with a very paternalistic government that provides excessive protection to its people. The NAFTA agreement in 1994 was the first challenge that the Mexican society faced bare bones. This event opened in a much faster pace Mexico to international competition, finding by itself in a very weak position, despite of the elements that where built in the agreement to help Mexicans to slowly catch the speed of the global market.

Paternalism implies that the people in Mexico ask for a lot of help from the government, while the global economy pushes to hold competition as a very strong force to develop the capabilities in each location. The NAFTA agreement pushed Mexican society to be much more competitive and asked to be more proactive. In the 20th Century the Mexican Diaspora was formed for low-income people that flew out from Mexico to become a bracero and provide their hand labor capability. From the end of the 20th Century and the beginning of the 21st Century the diaspora switched from the low cost labor to the master minds from Mexico that flew away to use the resources and opportunities from the Knowledge Society. This threat was a strong concern at the beginning of the 21st century and was called brain draining an issue associated with the highly qualified professionals.

A threat is always an element to be worried about; the government started to figure out how to slow down the rate that the highly qualified people left the country and explores the subject from the academic and research point of view. At the same time the civil society found that their families became separated while the sons and daughters started to go to get their degrees around the world. A fact that some left and stay away after they finished school, while others came back and bring new ideas, cultural issues and a lot of new opportunities.

 Suddenly the society switch from a paternalistic thinking to highly competitive attitude brought from the ones that came back as well to supported for the people that decided to live away. The change happen between 2015 to 2025, while a great number of people learn that the knowledge society opens the opportunity to develop his/her own capabilities in a challenging and changing environment when the new kind of jobs focused in how the human being can be more creative to develop new science, be very innovative and develop new products and services than enhance the human being. A trend that focus in the human side of us, instead of looking for focusing in the optimization to reduce the human participation derived from the post-revolution revolution to a more knowledge based economy where the focus is to find new ways to learn, develop and adjust to a fast changing world.

Social Transformation

For the Mexicans, that we have a strong links to Europe, that we love the good food, the art and the orientation to be humans within our family. This mix of environments where talking to people anywhere is available all the time, help us to create cultural movements center in the human being, the Mexicans realize that our creativity and history supported us to achieve any thing and the mindset freedom provided by the mix of our society with any other society in the world thru our diaspora, created a unique condition that reflected in new social trends.

The Mexican diaspora assimilate the new conditions faster that any other country, creating new government models, new educational conditions, new economic frameworks that where created abroad and landed in our country. The old concept of the 3 x 1 grants provided even at the beginning of the 21st century, become a new model of how ideas created anywhere, found resources to experiment in Mexico, developing the ocean border with new city models based in small self-contained towns capable to be Net Zero Energy facilities, where all the rubbish are recycled and the food is fully organic growth locally.

The mind shift changed in the following way:

From asking-to be supported and protected to making-new ways of everything, to end giving-away knowledge and support to people around the world.

The Mexican Presence

Three fields particularly have had a very strong Mexican presence:

Science, Creativity and Innovation. A great destination for Mexicans is to land in the universities and research centers to develop projects. Europe has been very open and supportive to bring people from around the world to develop state of the art projects looking how to advance the scientific subject further. Historically, Mexicans are very creative and innovative, then getting involved with the international community based in Europe foster their capabilities and expand their horizon to reach new levels. Examples of this are Luis Flores that was involved in the discovery of the Higgs boson in CERN, the European Organization for Nuclear Research in Switzerland; Xóchitl Domínguez Benetton that has been involved in electrochemical technologies and David Oliva related the brain surgery among others.

Entrepreneurship. Using the relationship with Mexico and the fostering of the entrepreneurship programs around the world, Mexican participate in their local places in developing multinational entrepreneurship lead by the United Kingdom that connected the programs with people in New Zealand, Guadalajara, Zacatecas and Boston to learn from each other. The learning process presented different platforms, cultures and capabilities in each location. Thru the diaspora, the learning process was improved based in the differences; the Mexican Diaspora was able to integrate different approaches into one using the Mexican creativity and innovation mindset.

Culture and Arts. The rich Mexican culture had been the platform to create new entertainment, writing and cultural developments becoming a reference to any other country. The mobility of the people that has been jumping from place to place as well as the great interaction among the Global Mexican Network using the technology available developed new concepts in how to keep a very cozy and intimate relationship despite the distance. Several social networks had used technology developed by Mexicans abroad that create better communications channels with a very high level of interaction despite the location of the people.

The discovery: we are in any place

A concern in 2005, when the Mexican Global Network born was to identify the best way to positioning Mexico in the minds of the people outside Mexico. A discovery to all the people involved in the challenge was to discover that Mexico was very much well positioned anywhere. It was a lot of great people working in subjects like: Education, Social Responsibility, Government, private companies and any kind of organizations that are available. This discovery brought the attention to the civil society as well as different entities in the Federal and State governments that instead of develop a positioning for Mexico was to move the Mexican people from the hideouts they leave to be a more active public people. This situation created a movement associated to the slogans "Made in Mexico" to

"Ideate in Mexico" to "Mexico in every place making changes and creating a better life"

This positioning created in the last 20 years by the Mexicans and around the Mexicans change the perception of a great country with natural resources, beautiful beaches and producers of great beer, tequila and mezcal to the place where great people live, believe and change the way we live everywhere. As the Millennia's generation think, Mexican people adopted the subject of Social Responsibility as a critical element to create a better world, the Mexican communities involve in education create a blend of cultures and education process that open the global education revolution associated with the knowledge economy where the people had needed to create new approaches to foster employment, to learn faster and focus into complete new way of thinking. The diaspora worked as a catalyzer that opened the frontiers not only to the geographical locations but also to the global mindset. The natural capability of the Mexican to be a social human being, started to generate new teams and clubs concepts getting together for subjects to learn about failure as the Failure Institute created in Mexico City after identify thru the diaspora that failing is a learning process and develop the FuckUp Nights that brought the opportunity to the people to present in public their failures in a way that they felt a relief of the bad experience and bring it as a teaching example to help people to succeed. Other groups developed new ways to learn faster, improve communication, develop creativity, empower people and develop leadership.

At the end, today in 2025

The Mexican Global Network is today a great example that people from a common place live everywhere, the roots and relations are getting strongest with the distance and the concept of brain circulation is a powerful resource to any country. In the current conditions, it is nice to have a great local neighbor, supported with a global interaction and having the possibility of being at home despite where we are located. This era is for the people capable to adapt and enhance whatever they do.

References

http://www.adnpolitico.com/opinion/2013/10/07/opinion-auge-migratorio#comentarios

https://en.wikipedia.org/wiki/Immigration_to_Mexico

[1] http://www.adnpolitico.com/opinion/2013/10/07/opinion-auge-migratorio#comentarios

[2] Jornadas Informativas que corresponden a las Reuniones Anuales de la Red Global MX
http://www.redtalentos.gob.mx/index.php?option=com_content&view=article&id=142&Itemid=206

15
Enterprising in the Creative Industry Sector

EDGARDO KOESTINGER*

*Managing Director Zédeo France, President of the Mexican Chamber of Commerce in France, Member, Member of Red Global MX France, Coordinator of Social Responsibility, Red Global MX Europe.

"Creativity is intelligence having fun"
-Albert Einstein

If we close our eyes for a moment and we think about what Mexico signifies the first immediate impressions we will get will be the typical clichés that everybody knows (tequila, sombreros, pyramids, mariachis, beaches, skulls, etc.). Then, if we go deeper in our thoughts and we open our eyes, we will find a much richer and wide vision and perspective of what Mexico really is. In fact, if we think twice we will discover that Mexican influence and creative industries are all over!

Nowadays several acclaimed Mexican filmmakers are shaking the cinema industry through their notorious talents. They have attained worldwide recognition thanks to their enormous filmmaking talent. Could we say that the fact that they are Mexicans has something to do with it? Probably yes. Besides their very hard work, tenacity and perseverance, the fact of having lived "Mexican experiences" living in Mexico has in a way shaped the way they conceived life and therefore the way they do movies.

I think I'm not exaggerating when I affirm that Mexicans have a natural creativity fruit of our ancient culture and distinctive identity shaped through plenty of different cultural influences. Our idiosyncrasy is as shiny and unique as an UFO in the open sky. This truth becomes evident when we think about the government commissioned visit to Mexico City of the French poet and writer André Breton, founder of the revolutionary cultural surrealism movement in the early 1920's. After visiting Mexico, André Breton discovered the city-sized open-air surrealistic gallery that is Mexico City. His understanding and comprehension of the Mexican creative expressions he discovered in Mexico make him affirmed that Mexico is the most surrealistic country in the world.

As Mexicans, we know what we are talking about. Sometimes even we don't understand why some things happen in a surrealistic natural Mexican way...

We can also make reference to the *magic realism* that Latin American writers used as a natural dream-like way of writing. The elements of fantasy and unreality that are present in their writings are as colorful, real and present as an "Alebrije" in the middle of a public park.

Photo of an Alebrije in the Parc de la Villette in Paris during the Mexican interactive exhibition "Le Mexique se vit à Paris" in july 2015 (photo: E. Koestinger).

How do we eat Creative Industries? A little bit of history...

"Disruptive innovation is entrepreneurs changing their industry with unique creativity." -Onyi Anyado

It's not easy to define what are the creative industries because even do they are several "official" definitions, there exists several and different approaches that difficult the task. Creative industries, because of their own natures are very vast, but the main criteria to define them has to do with the generated economic value through intellectual property creation.

The term *Cultural Industries* was born in Germany in the Frankfurt School during the 1930's to provide a name to the commodification of the art facing capitalism. Then by the 1980's the term was no longer pejorative and started to be used for policy making. At that time included art, music, writing, design, fashion, publishing, film production, radio and television. All these cultural activities produced a very important economic value that is considered part of the *Creative Economy*, which was a term popularized by the British writer John Howkins through his book: *"The Creative Economy: How people make money from ideas"*, published in 2001.

Howkins extended the cultural industries to science and technology (research & development, software and video games), and then, the term *Creative Industries* came along to cover the goods and services produced by the cultural industries, including those that depend on research and development and innovation, such as the software development.

The Department for Culture, Media and Sport of the United Kingdom (DCMS) started in the late 1990's a very important policy-making strategy to boost the economic development of their "creative cities", which is a concept of strategic urban planning that takes into account that creativity can change the economy and the society. This concept was popularized by the book *"The Creative City: A Toolkit for Urban Innovators"* written by the urbanist Charles Laundry in 2000. Laundry is the founder of the think-tank *Comedia* that studied the link between the creativity of his habitants and the transformation of their city.

After having adopted the "creative cities" concept, the "creative class" concept appeared in the book *"The Rise of the Creative Class"* written in 2002 by the American urbanist Richard Florida. His theory, even if it has been criticized by researchers and academics that found it elitist and more political than economical, supports the idea that the concentration of technology workers, artists and "high bohemians" foster an environment that attracts businesses and create economic development.

With the vision of these two concepts and the research report of the Policy Studies Institute *"The Economic Importance of the Arts in Britain"*, written in 1988 by John Myerscough, the government of the United Kingdom started to do some policy-making to encourage the potential of creative industries to booster jobs, revenues and domestic economy along with benefits from products and services exportation.

According to the DCMS Creative Industries Economic Estimates, the United Kingdom creative industries were worth £76.9 billion to the country economy in 2013 after growing by almost 10% each year. The sectors of architecture, crafts, design, games, publishing, museums, galleries, music, technology and television only, accounted for 1.71 million jobs in 2013, meaning 5.6 per cent of total UK jobs. These numbers can give us the idea of the importance of the creative industries for the economic development of a country and the importance for the world economy, as it is one of the fastest economic growing sectors.

The United Kingdom was one of the first countries to identify the potential of creative industries conceptualizing the idea along with policy-making to strengthening creativity and innovation as a strategic axis of its economy.

The official definition for *"Creative Industries"* of the DCMS is *"Those industries which have their origin in individual creativity, skill and talent and which have a potential for wealth and job creation through the generation and exploitation of intellectual property ".*

Event do they exist several classifications for the creative industries, the most commonly used is the DCMS model: advertising; architecture; art and antiques market; crafts; design; fashion; film and video; music; performing arts; publishing; software; television and radio; video and computer games.

Other classification and models are compared in the *Creative Economy Report 2013* published by the UNESCO (United Nations Educational, Scientific and Cultural Organization), in order to provide a better understanding of the creative and cultural activities that are constantly evolving according to different complexity contexts. The UNESCO definition for Creative industries is: *"sectors of organized activity whose principal purpose is the production or reproduction, promotion, distribution and/or commercialization of goods, services and activities of a cultural, artistic or heritage-related nature."*

The Australian cultural economist and Professor David Throsby, developed a model of comprehension of the creative industries through concentric circles based on their cultural and social expression.

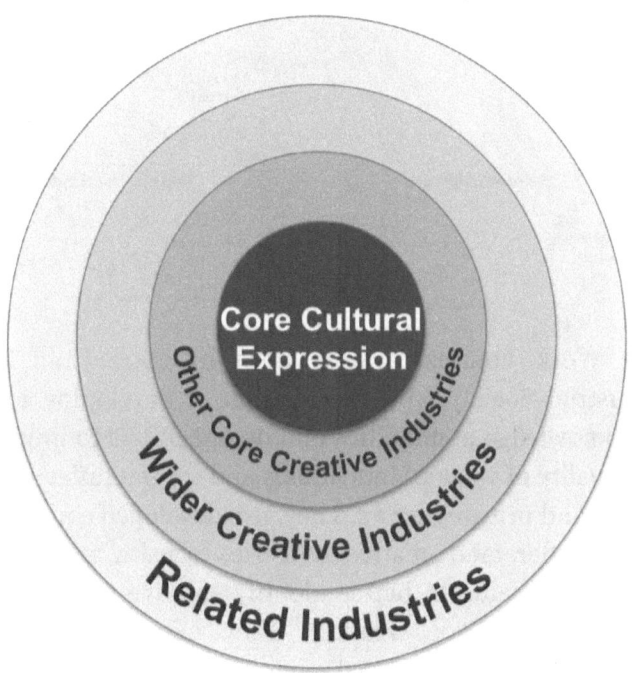

Professor D. Throsby Concentric Circles Model

Professor D. Throsby identifies different creative industries in successive circles according to their hierarchy of creativity as a social process. From the core cultural expression produced by creative workers in the center of the cultural value chain, to the services provided by art entrepreneurs, art producers and artists managers.

D. Throsby Cultural and Creative Industries Classification

Core cultural expression	Other creative industries
• Literature	• Film
• Music	• Museums
• Performing arts	• Galleries
• Visual arts	• Libraries
	• Photography

Related industries	Wider cultural industries
• Advertising	• Heritage services
• Architecture	• Publishing and print media
• Design	• Television and radio
• Fashion	• Sound recording
	• Video and computer games

The Work Foundation was born in 2002 from The Industrial Society with the mission of developing ideas and knowledge about cities and organizations to improve the quality of work of individuals and communities in the public and private sectors. They also developed a model to better understand creative industries focusing on the core expression value to better identify creative content and different fields of creation. They take into account aesthetic, spiritual, social, symbolic, authenticity and historical values as the notion of property and copyright as an important part of the creative economy.

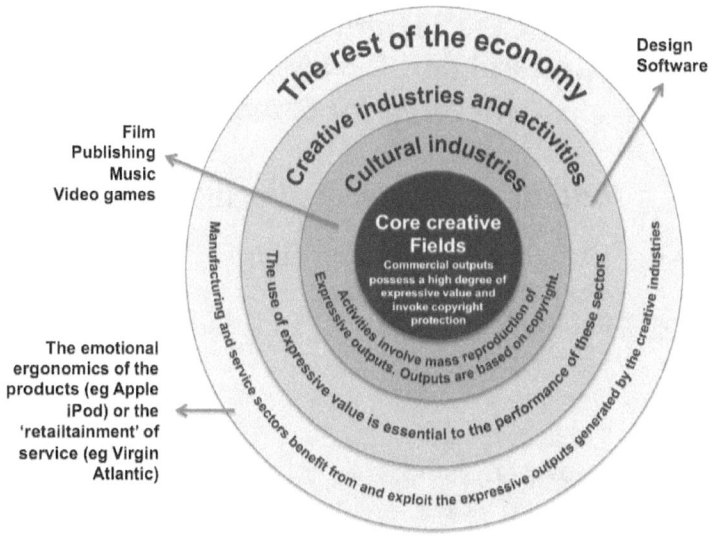

Film
Publishing
Music
Video games

Design
Software

The rest of the economy

Creative industries and activities

Cultural industries

Core creative
Fields

Commercial outputs
possess a high degree of
expressive value and
invoke copyright
protection

Manufacturing and service sectors benefit from and exploit the expressive outputs

The use of expressive value is essential to the performance of these sectors

Expressive outputs. Outputs are based on copyright

Activities involve mass reproduction of

generated by the creative industries

The emotional
ergonomics of the
products (eg Apple
iPod) or the
'retailtainment' of
service (eg Virgin
Atlantic)

The Work Foundation's Concentric Circles Model

For statistical, policy-making and property/copyright purposes there exist other classifications systems as the ones of the UNESCO Institute for Statistics and the WIPO (World Intellectual Property Organization) Creative Industries Copyright classification.

**UNESCO Classification System for
Cultural and Creative Industries**
Institute for Statistics

Industries in core cultural domains

- Museums, galleries, libraries
- Performing arts
- Festivals
- Visual arts, crafts
- Design
- Publishing
- Television, radio
- Film and video
- Photography
- Interactive media

Industries in expanded cultural domains

- Musical instruments
- Sound equipment
- Architecture
- Advertising
- Printing equipment
- Software
- Audiovisual hardware

World Intellectual Property Organization (WIPO) Cultural and Creative Industries Classification

Core copyright industries

- Advertising
- Collecting societies
- Film and video
- Music
- Performing art
- Publishing
- Software
- Television and radio
- Visual and graphic art

Interdependent copyright industries

- Blank recording material
- Consumer electronics
- Musical instruments
- Paper
- Photocopiers
- Photographic equipment

Partial copyright industries

- Architecture
- Clothing, footwear
- Design
- Fashion
- Household goods
- Toys

With this brief historical explanation of the origins, conceptualization and classification of the cultural and creative industries, it will be easier to explain what is the actual status of creative industries in Mexico. Also it is possible to imagine the benefits in the short and long term of adopting them as a strategic axis to promote jobs and welfare.

Where are we? Is Mexico really a creative nation?

For Mexico, the gateways of economic development opportunities through creative industries are wide open due to the inherent creative gene that is well rooted in our idiosyncrasy. We have creativity as one of the profound signals of identity of Mexicans because our way of being, and is very well known that we are creative in our way of working too.

Actual Mexican booming creativity extends not only to cinema, but also to other creative industries such as design, fashion, architecture, publishing, digital programming and audio visual content production. Cinema has been recently one of the must prominent proofs of Mexican talent in worldwide news, but actually there is a lot much more happening!

According to the UNESCO Creativity Report 2013, while countries like Argentina, Brazil, Chile, Colombia and Cuba have already a creative economy framework; Mexico is still in the process of adopting a permanent policy-making model in order to build the legal framework to promote creative industries at all levels. That's why Mexico's government is working with the triple helix (government, industry and academy) with a priority approach. The "creative class" theory of Richard Florida mentioned above, along with the strategic design, that is based on the "architecture of the problem" are at the heart of the Mexican government strategy to develop the creative industry sector.

To start designing the road map and start a consistent policy making strategy to booster Mexican creative industries, the Mexican government has adopted the creative economy definition in the *Creative Economy Report 2008* UNCTAD (United Nations Conference on Trade and Development) which states: *"The creative industries are the cycles of creation, production and distributions of goods and services that use creativity and intellectual capital as primary inputs; constitute a set of knowledge-based activities, focused on but not limited to arts, potentially generating revenues from trade and intellectual property rights, comprise tangible products and intangible intellectual or artistic services with creative content, economic value and market objectives; are at the crossroad among the artisan, services and industrial sectors; and constitute a new dynamic sector in world trade."* The UNCTAD summarizes in the report what the creative economy really is and what really means to the world economy: *"is the interface among creativity, culture, economics and technology, as expressed in the ability to create and circulate intellectual capital, has the potential to generate income, jobs and export earnings while at the same time promoting social inclusion, cultural diversity and human development".*

The Mexican government strategy is to implement clusters and strategic design as the axis to booster Mexican creative economy. This is why design in all its forms took a very important role for Mexico as the first spearhead of the creative industries development strategy.

In 2013 ProMéxico (the Foreign and Trade investment Office of the Mexican Government), published the document *"Ecosistemas de Diseño, Estrategia Nacional"* (Design Ecosystems, National Strategy). In this document, the strategic design is revealed as one of the most important tools that the government is utilizing to vitalize Mexican creative industries. Strategic design must take into account 3 factors according to the concept precursors of Helsinky Design Lab. These factors are: 1) Must listen to everyone involved in the problem that has to be solved. From the "C" executives or the taking decision team to the lowest range workers. 2) Visualize the problem with a diagram. The idea is to build a visual representation of the program to try to get a holistic point of view of it. 3) Once everyone has given his insight of the problem and once every possible solution is taken into account, the third step is to be certain of the feasibility of the solution in realistic terms.

In the ProMexico's national strategy document a SWOT analysis is presented to identify the problems, opportunities and solutions to booster strategic design as an economic development axis. A focus team was created with the most prominent Mexican designers and leaders of the design sector and 7 strategic projects resulted from this analysis with a horizon 2012-2016:

The creation of a Directory of Mexican designers

Create the National Council of Mexican Designers

Creation of the "Prix National of Strategic Design"

Itinerant Exhibition of Mexican Design

Promote Puebla as World Capital of Design

Create the "Design in Mexico" trademark

Write the "Mexican Design Positioning Working Plan"

These projects that are now achieved or in process are reshaping and vitalizing the Mexican design sector. Mexican designers are also very enterprising; they are doing their best to showcase their talents at an international level. As a sample of this it's important to mention Design Week Mexico as one of the most dynamic initiatives in Mexico that promotes design as a tool for social change. They are doing an excellent work to showcase the best of Mexican design talent through their project "Territorio Creativo" (Creative Territory). This project seeks to promote the best of Mexican contemporary design, highlighting designers that utilize typical Mexican materials transformed through innovation and creativity into world-class design products.

Other important initiative between designers, universities and enterprises related to design is the Abierto Mexicano de Diseño (AMD) (Mexican Design Open). To reveal the importance of the Mexican design sector is very relevant to mention that the Spanish edition of the UN Creative Economy Report 2013 was launched in Mexico City during the 2014 Mexican Design Open event.

In fact, this uprising appreciation of the quality and capacity of Mexican designers is recognized internationally. For example, recently, the International Council of Societies of Industrial Design (ICSID) named Mexico as World Design Capital for 2018. The biennially awarded cities that receive this nomination are designated thanks to their commitment of using design to promote cultural, social and economic development.

The panorama of design in Mexico has changed a lot in the last few years and also the way of teaching it, now the academy has created a real synergy with the industry.

The new generations of designers need a new approach of learning much faster and adapted to the changing world avid of solutions and products that reflects a lifestyle. The Centro University in Mexico City gives the skills that are taught to students by professionals, so the students are in contact with the industry needs and trends. Also, the creative atmosphere of the Centro University invites them to learn to live "creatively" and to follows one's creative drives and intuitions, which are at last, the best way to express in work!

The Design Fest that takes place in Guadalajara, Mexico, organized by REDiseño is an excellent showcase of the Mexican talent, and the Quorum Prix has been an excellent way to promote and reward the Mexican talent in different disciplines related to design

Also is important to mention Benito Cabañas, Director of Abracadabra design studio. He is one of the most recognized and influent Mexican graphic designers and he leads the "Coordenada 21" Designers Association in the city of Puebla, Mexico. This association is a group of design professionals that work to highlight the economic, social and environmental develop that is added to society through design. Benito and his group are working hard to reach UNESCO's designation of Puebla as World Capital of Design.

Mexico is internationally recognized as a country full of ancient history and modern influences. With its 1,209 museums, 1,782 Cultural Centers, more than 45,000 archaeological sites, the biggest cinematographic industry of Latin America, more than 10 international cinema festivals and 31 sites nominated UNESCO's world heritage, it is evident that Mexico has a tremendous rich cultural heritage to offer as a source of inspiration.

This year, The Leading Culture Destination Award known as "the Oscars of Museums" has recognized the "Gran Museo del Mundo Maya" in Yucatán, México, in their 2015 nominations.

The use and appropriation of Mexican cultural heritage and craftsmanship to revitalize and mix with modern materials has also reach the Mexican fashion industry. Some recognized designers as Carmen Rión and Lydia Lavín, or brands as Pineda Covalín have been working with typical Mexican designs and traditional textiles since several years, and nowadays, a much bigger group of brands and designers as Ricardo Seco, Yacampot, Arroz con Leche, Cihuah, Lorena Saravia, Carla Fernández, René Orozco, and much others, are transforming even the domestic market because they have become fashionable and trendy to Mexican fashion consumers too. The basic "made in Mexico" has left the folklore behind and has evolved to the design, created, innovated and manufactured in Mexico with world-class quality. Now is normal to see Mexican handcrafts in the MoMA (Museum of Modern Art of New York) store, or Mexican designed clothes in the *Global Fashion Capitals* collection of the Museum at the Fashion Institute of Technology.

I personally work in the creative industry sector doing fashion accessories designed by my wife. She has worked several years with the famous French fashion designer Jean Paul Gaultier, and we have developed together the brand Zéphyr & l'Olivier ® as a mixture of Mexican inspiration and French savoir-faire. The handbags that we sell are made in Mexico with the plastic fiber that my father started to produce in the 50's. Now my sister Margarita runs the family business and that's why the bag carries her name. We try to highlight the Mexican creativity through the designs and at the same time, we adapt them to the French market.

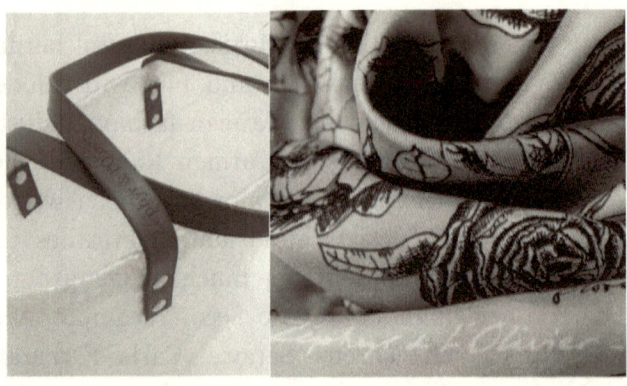

Transparent Margarita hand woven tote bag and detail of a 100% silk scarf from Zéphyr & l'Olivier ®

According to ProMéxico's publication *Mapa de Ruta - Industrias Creativas 2013* (Roadmap of Creative Industries), the creative industries represents the 7% of the worldwide GDP and they will have a constant growth of two digits in the next coming years according to the BID (Banco Interamericano de Negocios). Also, the PwC report *Global Entertainment and Media Outlook 2014-2018*, mentions that Mexican media entertainment and communications will increase 7.3% by 2018 with a forecast average turnover of 35.2 billion USD.

According to the Creative Economy Report 2010 of the UNCTAD, Mexico ranks the eighteenth position as the creative goods and services producer in the world, and leads the ranking in Latin America.

One of the most profitable and fast growing markets for the Mexican creative industries is the digital content production. Mexico has a lot of potential in this field as for example; a minute of animation (motion graphics) for publicity made in Mexico is less expensive than a minute of animation made in China, India or Russia. Mexico's soap operas (known as "telenovelas") are known worldwide thanks to the Mexican television companies Televisa and TV Azteca, as they are the largest producers and exporters.

MIPCOM (Marché Internationale de Programmes de Communication) in English: International Market of Communications Programs is a trade fair that takes place annually in Cannes, France, as the marketplace for televisions, broadcasters and studios. Thanks to the governmental support through the financial aid of ProMéxico, in 2013 only 12 Mexican companies were present in the MIPCOM, against 105 Mexican companies in 2014, as Mexico was the MIPCOM country of honor. This nurtured Mexican presence was an incontestable proof of the creative industry support as a governmental priority. The companies present in MIPCOM were selling television content, animated content, films and related services as visual effects, subtitles or dubbing.

During the MIPCOM Emilio Azcárraga Jean (CEO of Televisa) presented Televisa's latest innovation for interactive content creation. The technical and the creative aspects were very impressive showing the potential utilization of a second and a third screen that can became part of the TV show making possible in a near future to use the tablet or the smart phone as a side-line screen to watch the TV show. Unfortunately, the content that he presented as "Log Out" was an apology of violence in Mexico, not very comforting to look at, but very profitable to sell.

All these facts can show us the status of Mexican creative industries. We can still found very illustrative examples in architecture, photography, programming and video games. As significant data, Mexico has more than a hundred animation studios for video games and animated publicity. In art, it is worthwhile to mention that the Zona Maco Contemporary Art Fair, is the biggest art fair in Latin America with more than 120 galleries from 22 countries in its more than 12,000 square meters of exhibition.

This is an evidence of the constant growing Mexican art scene, and also a clear indicator of the constant increase of Mexican international presence in the creative industry arena.

The future of creative industries in Mexico

"L'avenir a beaucoup de noms. Pour le faible, c'est impossible. Pour la peur, l'inconnu. Pour les courageux, c'est la possibilité" -Victor Hugo

Mexico is already on its path to become a world leader in creative industries, as it is already the leader for Spanish content production. Definitely, our culture is our best ambassador and we have to hold to it as the best business card we could offer to the creative industries consumers, this means, all of us!!

Mexican writer Carlos Fuentes used to say that we could step aside from the third world thanks to our first world culture. I do believe this is true. Also I believe that all Mexicans working in the creative industry sector are aware of this, so we use our culture as an inexhaustible source of inspiration.

I have lived in Oaxaca, Mexico, which I consider one of the most fascinating states of Mexico thanks to its cultural diversity, and there I discover the delicious grasshoppers. Yes!! You can eat them. Then, living in France I have experienced myself that to create value you have to use creativity and adapt the products to the client's eye and taste. I proposed seasoned grasshoppers from Oaxaca, Mexico, to a well-known French enterprise specialized in exotic condiments, and after tasting them and being approved for the French gourmet foodies, a packaging was designed according to the enterprise's line of products image and I started to import them into France. These photos can give us the idea of the tremendous difference between selling grasshoppers in a market street in Mexico, and the change with the "delicatessen" presentation that a well-designed packaging does. This intelligent use of design is what creates value and builds a brand.

Grasshoppers sold in a street market

Grasshoppers sold in a gourmet grocery store

We have to appreciate, estimate and value the exceptional and unique things we have in Mexico that we can offer to the international markets adapting them to the target market.

At the moment when the countries were striving to reach the Millennium Development Goals, in the Creative Economy Report 2013 Special Edition Irina Bokova, General Director of UNESCO and Helen Clark, Administrator of the UNDP (United Nations Development Program) pointed out in their video message that *"Culture (...) is who we are, shapes our identity, is a means of fostering respect and tolerance among people, is a way to create jobs and improve people's lives, is a way to include others and understand them, helps preserve our heritage and makes sense of our future, empowers people ... works for development."*

We have to continue nourishing the "creative atmosphere" developed by the co-working spaces such as the Impact Hub or Laboratorio para la Ciudad (Laboratory for the City) in Mexico City, or initiatives as Creative Mornings and FuckUp Nights, and of course, events as the Bonus creative week or INCmty which held the Startup Nations Summit 2015.

All this events are awakening the creative gene of the Mexican youth and together they create the perfect environment for innovation and entrepreneurship.

A very special mention has to be made for the Ciudad Creativa Digital project (Digital Creative City) in Guadalajara, Mexico. This renovated space into the city of Guadalajara will concentrate a global node of audio visual, digital and interactive production for the Hispanic market. It will strengthen Mexico's position as the leader in Spanish content and it will become the most important cluster of creative industries in Mexico. Thanks to its geographical position it will reactivate a local economy, create a sustainable social development model and empower Mexico's position in the world creative economy.

In the direction of promoting entrepreneurship, the most important governmental initiative is the *Semana Nacional del Emprendedor* (Entrepreneur National Week), organized by the INADEM (Instituto Nacional del Emprendedor) (National Entrepreneur Institute). This event is boosting the Mexican entrepreneurial ambiance thanks to the important speakers that are invited to attend and the wide range of start-up's and business incubators and accelerators present in the event.

One of the most important key factor of success for the development of Mexican creative industries is the quantity of young Mexicans studying creative industries related professional careers. In the next coming years, all these new-born professionals will create their own enterprises and they will create, need and demand also products and services, but on this occasion, they will be accustomed to high quality products and services with global competitiveness.

Conclusion

"La verdad es que mientras más enojado estoy con este país y más lejos viajo, más mexicano me siento." -Jorge Ibargüengoitia (Instrucciones para vivir en México)

Until now I have described the concept of creative industries, explained briefly what is happening in Mexico these days and describe the way the Mexican government is building a framework and creating the conditions to booster creative industries.

Now, with a 2025 horizon I could affirm that it's a very exciting time for Mexican creative industries. Mexico will surely become a world leader in creative industries production if we keep on working together in a coordinate manner: creative professionals, government, academy and industry.

As mentioned above with the grasshopper's example, it's very important to adapt Mexican products (and services) to international markets exigencies without losing Mexican identity. The harshness and strictness imposed by actual global economic constraints surely intimidate Mexican companies to do business abroad, but we have to learn better how to sell our products and export our creative goods accentuating their Mexican origin. We have to adapt them to the business codes and quality standards needed to penetrate effectively international highly competitive markets. Mexican designers, even if they reshape traditional handcrafts with a more contemporary design have to be in compliance with international standards accompanied of competitive prices.

According to my experience, these are the kind of changes we have to start doing to promote Mexico efficiently. Our unique selling proposition must be our Mexican national identity but traduced in a world-class product.

What do we have to do to be more creative? The answer is obvious, we have to be more Mexicans, but with a universal approach understanding Mexico as an endless source of inspiration full of contrasts. We have learn how to transform with creativity our natural tendency to involuntary surrealism, into a fantastic high tech quality product.

All industry in general is paying more attention to creativity and innovation; it has been proof that they are essential for business growth and those enterprises that doesn't inscribe them in their business DNA will perish sooner or later. That is why we, Mexicans, with our creativity gene are very well positioned to face the future of all industry, and specially, the creative industry.

The UK government, being the first one in conceptualizing and building a legal framework to develop creative industries in order to create welfare, gives us the example of 5 areas to focus to continue developing creative industries in the best possible way, they are:

Developing infrastructure; education and skills; intellectual property; international exports; inward investment, considering three things that are vital to the long-term implementation of successful creative industries policies: data; cultural environment; innovation.

If we as a country keep on looking these factors closely, conjugating them with our Mexican creative gene and cultural identity, we will surely attain the objective of becoming a world creative industry leader.

I think Mexico is ready for this challenge. Let's be part of it!

References

[1] Alfonso Cuarón and Emmanuel "Chivo" Lubezki with "Gravity", Alejandro González Inárritu with "Birdman", Guillermo del Toro with "Crimson Peak", Amat Escalante with "Heli" and Michel Franco with "Chronic".

[2] The magic realism is a literary genre that uses mythical and fantastic elements to produce fiction novels.

[3] Fantastic and very colourful wood carved figure made in Oaxaca, Mexico.

[4] http://charleslandry.com

[5] http://martinprosperity.org/author/richard-florida/

[6] http://www.tandfonline.com/doi/abs/10.1080/10286630903029682?journalCode=gcul20

[7] https://www.gov.uk/government/news/creative-industries-worth-88-million-an-hour-to-uk-economy

[8] https://www.gov.uk/government/uploads/system/uploads/attachment_data/file/183544/2001part1-foreword2001.pdf

[9] United Nations Educational, Scientific and Cultural Organization, http://www.unesco.org/culture/pdf/creative-economy-report-2013.pdf and http://www.creativeeconomyreport2013.com

[10] http://www.businessandeconomics.mq.edu.au/contact_the_faculty/all_fbe_staff/david_throsby

[11] http://www.theworkfoundation.com/Aboutus

[12] http://www.uis.unesco.org/culture/Documents/framework-cultural-statistics-culture-2009-en.pdf

[13] http://unctad.org/en/docs/ditc20082cer_en.pdf

[14] http://www.promexico.gob.mx/documentos/mapas-de-ruta/MRT-Ecosistemas-Diseno-2013.pdf

[15] http://www.helsinkidesignlab.org/pages/what-is-strategic-design

[16] http://www.designweekmexico.com

[17] http://abiertodediseno.mx

[18] http://en.unesco.org/creativity/mr/creative-economy-report/spanish-edition-launch

[19] http://www.icsid.org/news/year/2015_news/articles2077.htm

[20] http://www3.centro.edu.mx/centro/

[21] http://www.design-fest.com

[22] http://rediseno.com

[23] http://www.quorum.org.mx/home/index

[24] http://abracadabra.com.mx/?lang=en

[25] http://www.promexico.gob.mx/documentos/mapas-de-ruta/MRT-Puebla.pdf

[26] http://www.lcdawards.com/awards/2015/#2015-destinations

[27] http://news.fitnyc.edu/2015/04/15/global-fashion-capitals/

[28] http://www.zephyretlolivier.com

[29] http://www.promexico.gob.mx/documentos/mapas-de-ruta/MRT-Industrias-Creativas-2013.pdf

[30] http://www.pwc.com/gx/en/industries/entertainment-media/outlook.html

[31] http://www.mipcom.com

[32] Ponencia de Emilio Azcárraga Jean en MIPCOM 2014: https://youtu.be/a3vfv1uknUk

[33] http://zsonamaco.com

[34] http://www.un.org/millenniumgoals/

[35]   http://www.unesco.org/culture/pdf/creative-economy-report-2013.pdf

[36] http://mexicocity.impacthub.net

[37] http://labcd.mx

[38] https://creativemornings.com/cities/mx

[39] http://fuckupnights.com

[40] http://bonusmx.com/wp/

[41] http://incmty.com

[42] http://ccdguadalajara.com/es_ES/

[43] http://semanadelemprendedor.gob.mx

[44] https://www.inadem.gob.mx

16

A fundamental competence: Curiosity and Wonder

CAROLINA ISLAS SEDANO, PH.D.*

Contextual Games expert in Educational Technologies, independent researcher and co-founder in Ubium Oy in Finland.

How does memory work? How does drinking water reach the upper floors of a skyscraper? Who or what lives in the deepest recesses of the ocean? What device should I develop if I want to charge my mobile phone by plugging it into a flowerpot? All these questions have already been be answered.

My primary intent in starting this chapter with questions above is to challenge you, the reader, to contemplate the question...***is curiosity important?***

What might this be? Food? A field? A roof? Plastic? Fabric? A craft? Wood? (Schweikert, 2011) .

Are you curious about the future?

My main research focus over the last 10 years has been the design and development of games, in particular contextual games. The main characteristic of contextual games is that their design involves explicitly different circumstances to that of the real world (e.g. environmental and socio-cultural elements) in which players will play these games. For example, imagine a game which is controlled by the weather conditions of a particular location. We have developed a game, entitled Heroes of Koskenniska (Islas Sedano, 2012), which does exactly this.

The factors which, in general, motivate players to finalize games include fantasy, competition and curiosity. We ascertained that *curiosity* is one of the main drivers which motivates players to finalize the contextual games which we design (Islas Sedano, et al. 2007).

Curiosity and *wonder* are also internal drivers which are needed in order to design and create these games. In actual fact, the advances made in science, innovation, arts and all that surrounds us, resulted from these authors embracing elements of curiosity and wonder. I have long since wanted to write about the importance of curiosity and wonder and the invitation to submit an article to "*The Future of Professional Fields: Views from the Mexican Diaspora in Europe*" presented the perfect opportunity to reflect on these topics and their importance in our society.

My preparation lead to the formulation of the following questions: *What is the Future of Professional Fields?* Do we know what those professional fields will be? At this point I must confess that I wholeheartedly subscribe to the reflections of Sir Ken Robinson (2008): "...*we have no idea what's going to happen, in terms of the future*".

It is easy to find evidence which supports Sir Robinson's statement. For example, a visit to any museum today will bear witness to professions that do no longer exist including that of rope-maker, weaver, watchman, tanner, ruffer or armorer. Even a cursory glance at the technology which surrounds you, for example your smartphone, will serve to prove Sir Robinson's statement. You might know that in the late 1970s, and early 1980s, mobile phones were not common gadgets and smartphones did not even exist. At that time no-one was talking about "apps developers". I was very privileged to learn BASIC, a programming language, in 1984 during a special course offered for children by the Universidad Nacional Autónoma de Mexico's Computer Center. In those years programming lectures aimed specifically at elementary or junior high school pupils were nonexistent in Mexico. I recall that some schools were trying to obtain computers to be used in computer classrooms as well as computer literate people who could teach the pupils. Often the computer classes at schools focused on understanding the commands of the current operating system (DOS) as Microsoft Windows did not exist at the time. Other things one learnt at computer classes in schools were word processing skills and how to navigate spreadsheets.

Today, in 2016, thirty-two years after my first exposure to programming, the world has changed. There is a global trend towards teaching programming at all school levels. Several countries have already created the necessary infrastructure and invested in human capital to enable the teaching of *programming* to students. This movement is giving rise to both opportunities and challenges in the area of digital development that did not exist thirty-two years ago. One might pose the question *how do you think programing will be in 10 or 20 years from now?*

Heraclitus (Joshua, 2010) stated that "*Life is Flux*" (*Panta Rhei* in Greek), meaning that all things are subject to change. Today we know that one of the few constants in life is, in fact, change. We also know that there is a considerable amount of things that we are not aware of. We know that societies are evolving and technologies are developing at a tremendous speed. Thus, everything is and will be subject to constant change. Are you curious about how the future will look?

What talents do you have that will help build our future?

You are probably quite curious about how our future will be. I find myself wondering what knowledge and talents do the reader possess which might help build our future *and* what type of future do we want to create. These questions are not posed to create feelings of anxiety within you, the reader, but rather to make you aware that we are creating our *new world* every moment of every day.

In September 2005 I started my doctoral studies at the Educational Technologies research group within the Computer Science department in Joensuu, Finland. At that time the university was called the University of Joensuu. Its name has subsequently changed to the University of Eastern Finland. Heraclitus was indeed right; all things do change. One of the reason why I selected this particular research group was because of their work in ICT4D (Information and Communication

Technologies for Development), i.e. research into how digital technologies can be utilized for development.

My research focused on games, because my passion is learning through playing. In the first years of my research few people were working in the area of games. In addition, the Finnish word "peli" (game), as used in my research in 2006, refers to games exclusively played by children while my aim was to refer to games suitable to all age groups. After a decade, the research into games has grown in both the number of researchers as well as importance. Today "peli" refers to games suitable to all age groups, from children to the elderly. As I mentioned before, things are certainly changing, constantly.

Why focus on games for learning? My main driving force has been México, and more specifically, Mexicans. We are a playful nation! In addition, I am aware of the importance of learning and how difficult it can be to attain access to education. I had to face this reality when I was forced to interrupt my studies, due to economic reasons, including a devaluation of the peso. I thus have first-hand experience of how important it is to have access to education, to promote learning, to nurture curiosity and to wonder in on our "free" time. There are many people who cannot finish their formal schooling but this, in no way, means that they cannot or that they do not want to learn. We should offer opportunities to continue personal development, independent of age, even if one cannot attend a school.

As I am writing this, things are changing dramatically and constantly in terms of access to information. Thanks to the internet, information can now be found in many formats and through many methods, including free lectures on the internet with MOOC (Massive Open

Online Course). However, we should remember that *information* is not necessarily *knowledge*. One has to personally process information to transform it into knowledge. My focus on contextual games supports the transmission of information, through playing, and so simultaneously creating knowledge while playing. My research can thus be subscribed to the area of informal learning.

What is informal learning? Let me explain briefly. In 1996, the ministers of education of the countries belonging to the Organization for Economic co-operation and Development (OECD) agreed to develop strategies for "lifelong learning for all". These strategies included three types of education: formal, non-formal and informal learning (OECD 2010).

Formal learning refers to organized education as offered in schools, training systems, etc. When viewed from the learners' perspective, the learning is intentional. They go to school to learn, or an employee attends a training course offered and organized by his employer.

Non-formal learning is also organized, but it offers the learners some flexibility. Non-formal learning is often organized through an initiative of the learners, or as an independent by-product of organized activities whether or not these activities have learning objectives as a goal. For example attendance of yoga classes, or a technology club.

Informal learning is never organized and it often makes use of learning through experience. The learner is exposed to different situations (e.g. at work, home or in his leisure time) and s/he learns something from the it.

However, we should not limit ourselves to the previous definitions, as Carreño Cardozo, Rodríguez Cortés and

Uribe Sarmiento (2014) state, we are constantly learning. Given that we are learning all the time, what are the roles of curiosity and wonder?

What are the roles of curiosity and wonder in new societies?

Curiosity and wonder are not the same thing, even if they are related. Curiosity refers to inquisitive thinking involving exploration, research and learning. It is closely related to the desire to acquire knowledge and skills. Wonder, on the other hand, is an emotion comparable to surprise, something that is unexpected but it is not threatening. Wonder is closely linked to curiosity and it is the main driving force behind most intellectual exploration. For many centuries, curiosity was either forbidden or curbed in our societies (Ball, 2013). An example of this is the era of the obscurantism where access to knowledge was deliberately restricted.

We, however, now live in a different world where information and knowledge is not enclosed or restricted to one person or one institution. Depending on the country's development we now operate at the intersection of three types of societies: Information Society, Knowledge Society and Smart Society.

Information Society is a post-industrial society in which Information Technology (IT) transforms every aspect of our cultural, political and social life. The main focus of this society is the production and distribution of information.

Knowledge Society is based on the creation, dissemination and utilization of information and knowledge. It is a society with an economy in which knowledge is acquired, created, disseminated and applied to enhance　　economic and social development

Smart Society will make more intelligent use of technology, people and resources for improved urban management.

In these mentioned societies, learning is a central aspect, although we still do not fully understand how learning takes place. Furthermore, the importance of innovation in these societies is evident, especially in the area of economies. One possible approach to promote innovation is by merging knowledge and creativity to produce new concepts, products and services.

In recent discussions with my colleagues, from industry and academia, regarding topic how we can support individuals to succeed in these new societies, we reached the following consensus: **we need people that can be curious and who are able to wonder.**

People have almost boundless access to information from which they can gain knowledge, and thus develop the tools and resources they need to succeed. But if people are not curious and they do not wonder, they will not be motivated to attain any type of information. They will mainly consume.

Our societies need individuals who are able to find their talents and who will identify problems which need solving. Curious and wonder-filled they will look in order to solve, all the while shaping our tomorrows. Unfortunately, we know so little about curiosity and wonder that we have many more questions than we have answers: How can we develop curiosity? And wonder? How can we promote it? How can we feed it? Where do curiosity and wonder reside? There is much work to do and every community and society must promote curiosity and wonder.

In summary, all of us contribute to and build the future, every single day. In this process being curious and being filled with wonder have a very important, and even pivotal role, to play. Those individuals who are able to harness their ability to be curious and to wonder, and who decide to grow in their own particular area of interest whilst developing their own talent, will excel. Furthermore, countries with citizens who are able to excel, based on their curiosity will, in the future, lead the way. As Albert Einstein stated: *"The important thing is to not stop questioning. Curiosity has its own reason for existence. One cannot help but be in awe when he contemplates the mysteries of eternity, of life, of the marvelous structure of reality. It is enough if one tries merely to comprehend a little of this mystery each day."* (1955).

References

Ball, P. (2013) Curiosity: How Science Became Interested in Everything

Carreño Cardozo, J.M., Rodríguez Cortés, A. B. and Uribe Sarmiento, J.J. (2014) Recreación, Ocio y Formación. Editorial Kinesis.

Einstein (1955) "Old Man's Advice to Youth: 'Never Lose a Holy Curiosity.'" LIFE Magazine (2 May) p. 64"

Islas Sedano, C., Laine, T.H., Vinni, M. and Sutinen, E. (2007,November). Where is the answer?-The importance of curiosity in pervasive mobile games. Paper presented at the ACM Future Play Conference. Retrieved from http://portal.acm.org/

Islas Sedano, C. (2012). Hypercontextualized Games (Doctoral Dissertation). Retrieve from Publications of the University of Eastern Finland. Dissertations in Forestry and Natural Sciences., no

79. Retrieved from http://epublications.uef.fi/pub/urn_isbn_978-952-61-0865-0/index_en.html

Joshua, J. M. (2010, July 14).Heraclitus of Ephesus. Retrieved from http://www.ancient.eu/Heraclitus_of_Ephesos/

Robinson, Ken. (2006). Sir Ken Robinson: do schools kill creativity?, TED Ideas Worth Spreading. Retrieved at May 18, 2008, from the website https://www.ted.com/talks/ken_robinson_says_schools_kill_crea tivity?language=en

OECD (2010) Recognising Non-Formal and Informal Learning Outcomes, Policies and Practices. Retrieved from: http://www.oecdbookshop.org/en/browse/title-detail/?ISB=9789264063846

Schweikert, C. (Photographer D40OOM). (2011.11.19). Fontains blanket [digital image]. Retrieved from www.d4000m.eu

17

The future of Offshore Exploration

ANTONIO AMADOR*, FEDERICO JUAREZ**

*Geologist, Suncor Energy.

**Well Integrity Engineer at ConocoPhillips.

The year 2015 was a challenging year for the oil and gas industry. For many, the top of oil investmelbania2onts had been reached by the end of 2014 (DnB, 2014) (E&Y 2014) and less investment in upstream sector of the oil industry was foreseen for both 2015 and 2016.

Since the second half of 2014 when oil prices dropped, the industry has been challenged by low oil prices, big volume of oil supply in the market and projects turning into unprofitable assets. North America's oversupply has currently brought oil prices down. In 2015, the big surprise has been the lift of the sanctions imposed on Iran from the U.S. and the West. The Mexican oil reform also opened new possibilities for the development of more petroleum fields and increase the recovery in some of the world's biggest.

The petroleum activity contributes substantial value to the world's economy every year, and has created very important value in the global economy since it began. Big revenues help to create economic security and jobs nationwide. Petroleum operations have been under way since long time ago, and forecasts indicate that profitable production and a high level of activity will continue for many decades to come.

The main objective of the petroleum exploration is the study of the geological hydrocarbon bearing formations through different advanced technologies that help to better predict the discovery of new oilfields. Additionally, its purpose is to get more accurate estimations of the reservoir conditions in order to optimize the budget expenditures in drilling and construction of oil facilities.

The petroleum exploration is responsible for evaluating all parameter uncertainties related to oil discoveries which have direct implications for the oil extraction. Therefore, a proper production facilities design depends on the interpretation accuracy of the Geology & Geophysics analysis that can reach for a better characterization of the oilfield reservoirs.

The exploration activities consist of several phases, such as:

Sedimentary basin analysis: Study of the history of the basin fill related to the deposit, maturation and oil expulsion of the hydrocarbon source rocks.

Petroleum system analysis: Study of elements and processes of petroleum geology, including the source, reservoir, seal, and overburden rocks, and processes such as trap formation, generation-migration-accumulation.

Play analysis: Study of one or more geologically related prospects charged from the same source rock.

Exploration opportunities analysis: Visualization and dimensioning of the prospective areas, and identification of the main petroleum system uncertainties.

Prospect evaluation: Study of a potential trap that must be evaluated by drilling to determine whether it contains commercial quantities of petroleum.

Wildcat well drilling: First well in the selected area which test the prospect and guide the exploration. The result can be a dry hole or a well discovery.

Ultimately, volumetric estimates of OOIP and OGIP are based on a geological model that geometrically describes the volume of hydrocarbons in the reservoir. The methodology for the assessment included a complete geologic framework description for each province based mainly on published literature, and the definition of petroleum systems and assessment units within these systems. Exploration and discovery history was a critical part of the methodology to determine sizes and numbers of undiscovered accumulations.

The main areas open for offshore exploration in the world are: West Africa & Africa; Caspian Sea; South East Asia; East Asia; Australia; Black Sea; North Sea Europe; Mediterranean Europe; Middle East Persian Gulf; Middle East Red Sea; North America-Canadian Arctic; North America-Canadian Atlantic; North America-Canadian Pacific; North America-Gulf of Mexico (U.S. and Mexico); North America-Alaska; North America-U.S. Atlantic; South America-Brazil; South America-Caribbean; South America-Venezuela; Arctic.

The big surprise for the year 2015 was the opening of the east Atlantic coast offshore U.S. More areas are expected to open for exploration in the upcoming years

The arctic is another important area of interest. Debates have been going during the last decade on whether this area should be opened for offshore drilling or be left closed. In the Arctic waters as a whole, an estimated 134 billion barrels of liquids and over 48 trillion cubic meters of natural gas remain to be discovered. This wealth of resources makes up a significant portion of future global supply. Since 1979 more than 100 exploration wells have been drilled in the Arctic waters, with many oil and gas fields being discovered (Hoeven, 2015).

From the countries with interest in the Arctic, Norway is the most advanced on offshore drilling. Still, further exploration and development drilling activity will be needed in order to enable production in coming decades. The United States, Canada and Greenland have their own offshore exploration projects, but are likely to face significant opposition on environmental grounds. This is understandable, as indeed any accident could have devastating impacts on sensitive Arctic eco-systems and any misstep by industry could end up postponing Arctic resource development for decades.

Development of areas like the Arctic will bring new technological and environmental challenges of high risk and with no margin for error.

There will be several factors influencing the development of offshore exploration: technology and innovation; climate change; policies and regulations; geo-politics; oil price; development of unconventional onshore oil and gas resources; enhances oil recovery of already developed and mature areas; technology changes and use renewables.

At present, it is common that the offshore discoveries are characterized by a number of small discoveries under evaluation. Most are expected to be developed with subsea solutions tied back to nearby fields.

Given the right decisions in a long-term perspective, good profitability can be achieved through the interaction between field and discovery. The latter can benefit from established infrastructure, while the field can have their share of costs cut, their producing life extended and work on improving recovery continued. Without good utilization of existing infrastructure, many of the discoveries will probably fail to be developed or bringing them on stream will be considerably delayed and cost more. In that case, fields will have to cease production earlier and the potential for improved recovery cannot be realized.

Recently, attention in the petroleum industry has concentrated on cost trends and profitability. Oil prices regulate the activity and the substantial willingness to invest. The consequences have been higher level of costs, with pressure on profitability as the result. If costs continue to be unstable, projects could be postponed or shelved.

Cost trends in the petroleum industry represent a challenge both for developing discoveries and for committing to projects which can improve recovery from fields. The gap between forecast and target is expected to be filled by implementing yet more improved recovery measures on the fields and by forthcoming developments delivering even better than planned.

Offshore Exploration will continue intensively in the Gulf of Mexico but in mature areas like the UK will decrease significantly. For example, Rystad energy expects oil price to increase by 2017 (Nævestad et al., 2015). This will bring back investment in areas like North America, UK and the NCS. Nevertheless, in some areas with low potential like the UK, it is still expected a significant reduction in Offshore Exploration. Here, exploration results have been persistently poor and in decline since activity peaked in 2007/2008 (121 wildcat and appraisal wells were drilled) and down to a historical low in 2014 (38 exploration wells drilled) due to lack of resources found.

Offshore exploration will continue on ten years from now but it will most likely decrease its interest in the Arctic area mainly because:

New unconventional resources are found onshore

New countries open up for private Oil and gas exploration and investment

Enhanced recovery of already mature areas.

Less oil demand in the mid-term future and a stable steady up offer in the markets.

However, situation can change in the long term. If, development of unconventional onshore resources proves harmful for human life and the environment, governments will most likely end up making Oil and gas upstream-related policies stricter, which would push Oil and gas companies into a different direction.

References

Brownfield, M.E., et al., 2012, An estimate of undiscovered conventional oil and gas resources of the World, 2012, World Petroleum Resources Project, U. S. Geological Survey.

Charpentier, R.R., Klett, T.R., and Attanasi, E.D., 2008, Database for assessment–unit analogs (exclusive of the United States), Version 1.0: U.S. Geological Survey Open-File Report 2007–1404, 36 p.

Norwegian Petroleum Directorate, 2014, Petroleum resources on the Norwegian Continental Shelf 2014, Fields and Discoveries, Annual report 2014.

Vincelette, R.R., Beaumont, E.A., Foster, N.H., 1999, Exploring for oil and gas Traps, AAPG Treatise in Petroleum Geology.

DnB. (2014). Økonomiske Utsikter. DnB Bank. DnB.

Hoeven, M. V. (2015). Norway's role in the global energy transition. Hentet fra IEA: https://www.iea.org/newsroomandevents/speeches/150420Norway_BarentsSeaConference.pdf

IEA. (2014). World Energy Outlook 2014. International Energy Agency.

Martinez, R. (2015). Mexico Opens its deepwater frontier to new exploration. Hentet fra Offshore Magazine: http://www.offshore-mag.com/articles/print/volume-75/issue-9/mexico-update/mexico-opens-its-deepwater-frontiers-to-new-exploration.html

18

E-Government Perspectives for Mexico

CARLOS IVAN VARGAS ALVAREZ DEL
CASTILLO*

E-Government Specialist at RaulWalter LLC, Phd Candidate at Tallinn University.

By analyzing the past and current initiatives related to e-government in Mexico is hard to create or to imagine a concrete future scenario. The perspectives fluctuate constantly as political parties and government priorities change, at least in the federal level. The other possible way to analyze e-government in Mexico is at local level in which the results seem to be more concrete and continuous.

In either both ways the political factors influence the outcomes and upcoming projects. The citizens' satisfaction doesn't seem to be a priority and private companies are the ones sustaining the model.

Of course it is not fault of the government, the citizens or private companies, at least not in a direct way. But then, what is happening that e-government is not giving results as remarkable as in other countries?

Throughout this paper an overview of the Mexican e-government history will be provided. Then an analysis of the current situation using as an example the Mexican Digital Passport project. Finally, perspectives and scenarios for Mexican e-government for 2025 and assessment of possible solutions.

Mexico into a new era. Digitalization and e-Government

Nowadays Mexico is considered to be one of the e-government and digitalization leaders in Latin America and the Caribbean. As result of that it holds the presidency of eLAC (Digitalization Plan for Latin America and the Caribbean) until 2018.

Even though Mexico holds these positions, it has not always been like that and its story of digitalization has been slow and bumpy.

The story of the inclusion of ICT in Mexican territory and its government started during the presidency of Mr. Ernesto Zedillo Ponce de Leon on the last years of the 90's.

The former president and his team created a Modernization Plan for Public Administration. This plan was innovative at the time for giving budget for the development of ICT at federal level, unfortunately the development of ICT consisted in providing computers to the public sector. Task that didn't quite solve any real issue or improved in a significant way the efficiency of the government.

For the presidential period hold by Mr. Vicente Fox Quezada the development of digitalization and e-government had a breakthrough. A special presidential commission for Innovation and Governmental Quality was created. During this period e-government is mention for the first time in Mexico and an interest in following the world trends of innovation was growing. Thanks to the investment and development that Mexico had during the mandate of Mr. Vicente Fox, Mexico is now located as one of the leaders in e-governance in Latin America.

Later on, unfortunate situations like the increasing development of organized crime in Mexico require to focus more resources and time to fight it during the mandate of Mr. Felipe Calderon. The progress of e-government therefore was slowed down and taken out of the priority list.

Since 2012 with the current mandate of Mr. Enrique Pena Nieto a new wave of e-government evolution has begun. Mainly fault of international pressure as e-government is consider the necessary tool to fight basic problems that countries in the world face. Problems like corruption, digital divide, inequality or illiteracy. E-government and its solutions represent an opportunity to fight and diminish these unwanted situations.

Moreover, the Mexican Presidency created the National Digital Strategy which aims to digitalize the country and offer new e-services. Mexico was assigned president of eLAC until 2018 and has in its hands the responsibility of showing the best models and solutions for e-government to the region.

What is happening?

E-government is all about simplicity hence the explanation for technical solutions are rather easy. Unfortunately, not the same thing happens with the situation that the development of e-government has in certain countries, in this case Mexico.

A lot of factors are involved; political system, political influence, power relations, international pressure, information or disinformation on the topic, economic interest... just to mention few of them.

In order to understand the current situation of the country first we have to have in mind the federal system of the country and the autonomy that states have in the matters of implementing e-government features and projects. As a result of this division and freedom for developing independent projects we can observe a non equal evolution of digitalization in the country.

This characteristic is not precisely negative as pilot project can be tested in smaller states and adopted on bigger ones diminishing the range of possible failure.

Said that, we have to mention another big factor; the solutions that are adopted for Mexico and where they came from. Later on, the case of the Mexican digital passport will illustrate better the consequences of adopting a such called "best solution".

To move forward in the explanation of what is happening in Mexico in the area of e-government we should understand what e-government means in Mexico. The concept in general has been subject to many interpretations around the world. Almost all international organizations dealing with e-government have a definition and if we change from country to country also the understanding of e-government changes. This situation complicates even more its development as all governments are trying to implement it but nobody seems to knows exactly what it means.

The intention of this paper is not to provide an answer to that interrogative, but it's important to have it in consideration at the time of evaluating the future of e-government in Mexico. There are some common basic elements among all definitions like the one providing e-services in order to simplify the tasks for the end users or using e-government to fight corruption and inequality. Also, that there should be a unique portal to access all services. These descriptions don't say much about e-government and if we analyze some Mexican governmental portals, the e-services are there, but in reality the end user still has to physically attend an office to complete a process.

So, based on the current situation in Mexico and the current public biddings, e-government is based on the elaboration of applications to solve specific needs. Also, the computerization of public institutions and the provision of basic services via internet.

In reality the novelties in the world could offer much more than that but the organization and models used for creating an e-Mexico are not the most reliable.

Due to the proximity and economic relation, one of our major models in e-government is the United States of America but their solutions involve a large monetary investment with not very efficient results.

Digital Passports: Evolution or Regression?

As previously mention, a good and current example of the incursions that Mexico has into the era of e-government is the digital passports offered by the Ministry of Foreign Affairs.

The first thing to clear out is that digital passport in Mexico means that you can apply for an appointment and make the payment online plus the biometric security that the passport itself has. Then the citizen has to go to the appointment and proceed with the interview and data gathering.

To create this technical solution that would simplify the process of obtaining a passport, the Presidential Office via the Digital National Strategy and the Ministry of Foreign Affairs spend 84 million dollars in giving a contract to the company "Veridos Mexico".

The intention was to have the project running by October 1ˢᵗ 2015 but the system failed and the delivery of digital passports was completely suspended with the major inconvenient that also the delivery of regular passports was compromised.

This situation led the government to a crisis that was kept unsolved for several weeks.

The official explanation was that the company was not able to fulfill the requirements and there would be investigations to find the responsible parts. Meanwhile, there was the necessity of reestablishing the services as soon as possible.

Finally, a new contract with unspecified budget was given to "Softtek" to give support to Veridos and regularize the issuances of passports.

Based on this short but illustrative example: what can we learn from the situation of e-government in Mexico? There are few interesting points that we have to follow to understand what is happening and what will happen in this area for the next ten years.

The data gathering for the passport was to be simplified by providing online documents. The reality is that with the available technology the government should have this information already in a database without having to ask people for it once again. The online payment and appointment should not be announced as novelty but rather consider as implicit due to the fact that these solutions have been in the market for the last 15 years.

The technical solution given to "Veridos Mexico". The main headquarters of the company are in Germany and Veridos Mexico is a collaboration of several enterprises. (Giesecke & Devrient, Informatica El Corte Inglés, NEC, IECSA México, CAELUM Group and Seguridata Privada) These companies have presence in Germany, Spain, Mexico, Poland, Portugal, Hungary and Belgium. From these countries not one single of them are recognized as best practice models for digital identity nor e-government solutions. So that raises the question of who are we copying models and solutions from. If Mexico doesn't implement proven success solutions the most probable thing is that it won't have successful results.

The contract to Veridos after failing and crashing the system that stopped the issuance of passports was kept instead of being canceled. Moreover, it was extended to another Mexican Company to give technical support, demanding a larger budget. Fortunately, the results have not been negative and the issuance is now regular although it cost more time and more money than expected.

The suspension of passports for few weeks left and open door for malicious users. The digital system and database were paralyzed and the issuance of emergency passports was made entirely by hand. This created a perfect opportunity for people in need of a passport to cover an identity as the falsification was easier than if checked by a digital program. Surprisingly no media nor the authorities covered the national security risks that this project had.

Independent efforts to digitalize specific needs drive away the attention to a unique solution that integrates all services in a single system. This means that there is a lot minor projects like the digital passport but not a single and unique project that covers all aspects of an e-government. As a consequence of this strategy a lot is being done but at the end nothing innovative or useful to society or to the government because it can't be connected to one another.

In conclusion, the implementation of a digital service in Mexico such as the digital passport turnout to have bigger monetary costs, bad results and no satisfaction for the end user. Characteristics completely opposite to the main bases of e-government. Of course this is only a case but it works as a good example to illustrate how e-government functions in Mexico. The government gives a contract to a company for solving a problem without the knowledge of whether these solutions works or not in other places and if these other places have a good experience with it. Furthermore, the next digital solutions that the government wants to take will be marked by failed first steps and it will be harder for the population to have a positive response to them creating a mistrust issue.

A matter of black and white

In technology there is not such a thing as relatively good or relatively bad. When machines and softwares have a task, they have two options: to achieve the task as it meant to or not. If the machines don't deliver the expected results, then it means they don't work.

Now, e-government is based on technology but is not as simple as the previous explanation as it involves machines and people in a single system. Therefore, the chances of failing are bigger as is not only responsibility of the technology used in a solution but also the human factor that affects the outcomes.

Even though the humans are not meant to be categorized as machines, we have to adapt to the system and shorten our range of mistakes or failure. This understanding of our collaboration in a system where we have to live hand to hand with machines has a name: E-government ecosystem.

For achieving the stage of ecosystem there is no other way than having the best solutions. The humans (decision makers and specialists) have to research on the best case models for benchmarking, then invest in the proven solutions and finally achieving results with the most advance technology in the market. Otherwise, as the previous example shows, a simple and common task can become a huge and expensive project.

Furthermore, that leaves us to the simple option of weather doing it in the correct way or in the bad one which will eventually have failures and risks of security and privacy. Unfortunately, there is no middle way in which it can partially work, at the end is matter of black or white.

Ten Years from Now

As mention previously in this paper due to the federal political system that Mexico has, the initiatives for achieving a fully integrated e-government come from local governments and from the federal government. E-government should not be considered as a tool for political popularity but instead as a policy that will bring benefits for Mexico as a whole. Said that, we can talk about possible scenarios in which Mexico develops e-government projects.

One scenario in case the federal and local governments collaborate to achieve a main goal would be the ideal one. The states would still keep their autonomy but they will work under one central system creating a positive pressure for other states less developed and to the federal government to follow a single pad. The result could be in case there is organization and good investment without corruption, a fully integrated e-government. Ten years is a feasible time lapse for arriving to this point. By having this result we could conceive a Mexico with a minimal amount of corruption and inequality helped by the development of technology.

Another scenario closer to reality and following the patterns until now, is that both federal and local government will continue with independent projects. Some of these projects will be successful some other not. The investment will continue to be excessive and with poor results like in the United States model. The success of some local governments will develop small smart cities randomly located in Mexican territory giving as result a bigger digital divide in the population. Eventually this successful cases would push other governments but the development will be slow and bumpy.

Another thing that is necessary for a good development is the education and research in this area. In the world there are countries that offer knowledge in the development of e-government like South Korea, Singapore, Israel or

Estonia. This models stand for the best solutions in the world with top experts that provide consultation.

Mexico has to learn that e-government is not only applications, is not e-services, is not e-banking and definitely not online appointments. E-government has a more holistic approach and its evolution has led to a complete structure that includes all the previous features as part of it among much more others like a secure digital identity and a united governmental/private data sharing system.

19

Legal Practice 2030

A vision of the future for legal practitioners

LANDER MICHEL ROSALES SEDANO*

President of the Mexican-Catalan Association and board member of the American Society of Barcelona.

The present pace of technology and current trends make for a plethora of future developments which will affect all industries and service providers as well as challenge basic precepts of how models and businesses operate. Legal practice will not be an exception even though it will be one of the industries less prone to be affected, in overall terms, owing to its fundamental structure which is a personalized service based industry of which people have a specific paradigm (i.e. we expect a lawyer to act, appear and speak a certain way). The purpose of the present is to focus on megatrends which are slowly being incorporated to a greater, or lesser extent, by the legal profession in different areas of the world.

Several basic premises have been taken into account for the basis of this article; the Asia-Pacific region will continue to develop and businesses and GDP weight of that region will continue to increase compared to other regions, development of emergent and disruptive technologies will propagate, new generations of consumers will be more willing to try both new technologies and break with the *status quo* concepts of business models in all industries and services, consumers will be more demanding while at the same time willing to spend less for the same basic product or service; this will create an opportunity for service providers which are able to bridge the gap between traditional and non-traditional services. The most significant trend over the next decade for this author is the advent of Artificial Intelligence (AI) as well as significant changes in practical biological applications.

Future law practitioners

Future lawyers will not only require a working proficiency of English but also be required to further specialize in their area of expertise. Furthermore, new industries will favor lawyers with a more scientific and technical background or knack for science and technology over those who lack technical knowledge. Significant advances over the course of the next decade in the fields of science and technology will create new opportunities for lawyers with the skill sets and knowledge required to understand these areas—many of which will not necessarily be regulated and which may not exist at present.

Therefore, upcoming and practicing lawyers should develop a five to ten-year plan to acquire specialist knowledge of a specific science or technology at a technical level; this familiarity will prove an influencing factor when being considered for a project and such preparation should not be taken for granted. Lawyers from nations without a strong science and technological background may be at a disadvantage with their peers.

Lawyers who are able to live in another jurisdiction and qualify in that jurisdiction will have an edge over those who do not; it is no longer sufficient to study abroad, legal practice in another country is now a necessity be it only as an intern. Successful lawyers will be qualified in other jurisdictions or, at the very least, to be able to have a network and understanding of other cultures. There will be a significant benefit for lawyers who are qualified in both a civil and common law system with significant market growth in the Asia-Pacific region with Africa rising as the second most important future growth market ahead of Latin America.

Lawyers who are able to speak Arabic, Chinese, Russian, Spanish, Farsi and Hindi will have a competitive edge over those who do not. Countries which will have a demand for qualified lawyers with dual-qualification are likely to be Russia, China, India, Mexico and Iran.

Legal Services Trends.

As regards the price of legal services the advent of AI in legal practice as well as outsourcing will have an impact on the price of legal services pushing the prices downwards for consumers and in turn will reduce the need, and amount, of lawyers required. This implies that many lawyers will need to do other activities in order to make ends meet. Full-time legal practitioners will be fewer in number than at present. Mid-size firms will be required to internationalize and thus there are opportunities for lawyers who can give added value, with cross-border, specialist knowledge. Technologies will also allow mid-size firms to take upon larger projects in other jurisdictions, via outsourcing, than would otherwise be possible. Current trends of alliances of loosely aligned firms will only strengthen overtime with a need to make alliances and lower cost structures as there will be less income flow for most firms.

Outsourcing of legal services to third countries and their legal practitioners' will increase significantly which will make contracting firms more competitive and able to have lean structures. In addition, AI will begin substituting the need to hire a lawyer for general legal advice as they will be able to tap into online resources and give sound advice which need only be certified by a lawyer in order to be considered legal advice. Thus prices for legal services will increase in complex cases but, at the same time, basic legal service fees will face a downward pressure as a result of the aforementioned use of AI and outsourcing. Notwithstanding, consumers will have to pay a premium for bespoke services. Law firms are likely to have leaner structures and more likely to hire professionals on a per project basis to reduce fixed costs.

AI as a Judge

At present we believe that a Judge is required in order to Rule on a case however, current technology trends and breakthroughs in AI related technologies (Big Data, Parallel Computation and better algorithms) imply that an AI will be more efficient than a Judge at assessing and giving a Ruling in particular as regards the speed of response of the AI. The AI will be able to analyze all previously ruled upon court-cases, in particular, those related to the case at hand as well in order to give a Ruling. This technology is likely to be applied to misdemeanors or an infraction in a criminal court and applied to other areas of law where the sums in dispute are considered minor. This technology will imply significant savings by the jurisdictions that apply them but will also require continued investments in IT security to prevent criminal manipulation of said systems as well as in the general roll-out of the technology.

Court Houses

The development of Virtual Court Houses where plaintiffs and defendants may interact and log on from secure environments without being required to travel to a physical location will enable significant freeing up of both physical assets and space currently allocated for the maintenance and security of Court Houses. In addition, AI use in the Court House will replace basic clerk services, allowing the AI to summarizing key legal arguments and facts of a case, analyze these and provide research regarding the legal background of this case compared with similar case rulings over time thus freeing the Judge and other judicial personnel from those tasks in order to offer a more efficient justice system.

Harmonization

Various trade agreements currently in effect and use by Mexico, as well as new or upcoming ones, will harmonize key legal concepts between Contracting States. This will create opportunities for those specialized in cross-border transactions. Cross-border networking will become a necessity. At the macro level legislation from different nations will also grant access to these specialists access to local markets.

AI and Legislation

Towards the mid-2020s AI will carry out research and other legislative tasks currently done by legal practitioners as well as legislative bodies. One key example would be research and cross comparison of all legal articles affected by a newly proposed or modified article. Change is likely to be very gradual in this area with trials regarding redrafting of an article, as well as affected articles, enacted by AI rather than a full-scope law being drafted.

AI and Civil Responsibility

There will be significant discussions regarding who is responsible for the actions enacted by AI in particular taking into account its capacity to learn from experience therefore allowing for elasticity, adaptation and deviation from original programmed parameters and guidance. This clear potential for infinite evolution in the development of AIs learning process will require clear definition of who is ultimately responsible for its actions; the company that created it, the programmers or the AI itself. Past experience with robots in Japan for example shows that some robots go rogue; this without considering that, in so far as is known, this despite the fact that none of the robots had advanced AI systems.

Conclusion

In conclusion legal practitioners will face a more competitive market than the current generation as we move to increasingly network centered and globalized world. Lawyers will be required to adapt and move within this new environment; understanding that there will be less need for full time practitioners to the extent that outsourcing, the use of AI and project based law contracts will limit the relative job security currently enjoyed. Those lawyers who prepare themselves for the long term and have specialist knowledge of technical areas will be better positioned to thrive in the future as well as be able to adapt to changes whereas a gap will only increase with those who lack or have limited technical knowledge.

20

Red Global MX: a 2020 Network

A collaboration model with organized civil society
abroad

FRANCISCO DE LA TORRE*, SOFÍA OROZCO
AGUIRRE**

*Consul of Mexico at Dallas, TX, USA.

***Director of Red Global MX at the Institute of Mexicans
Abroad.*

In today's global economy, human resources are paramount for competitiveness at the international level. This translates into a need for talent attraction policies in developed countries. In this context, the relationship between migration and development, as well as the economic ties of migrants with their country and communities of origin, have become more relevant in the discussion of development policies and must be present in public policies in the near future. The amount and importance of remittances is one of the main reasons for this phenomenon, especially when considering that the worldwide amount of remittances is higher than the total amount of money destined to international assistance. Another factor is the strategic importance of qualified diaspora and the increasing impact of technologies in what is now called knowledge societies. [1]

Several countries around the world have developed successful models that acknowledge the importance of keeping close ties with their diaspora. The World Migration Fund recently offered an opportunity to renew the debate around the scientific, technological and entrepreneurial initiatives of the diaspora. In 2015 it recommended measures such as establishing vast agreements among the private sector, governments, civil society and non-profit organizations with entrepreneurs and migrants in order to facilitate entrepreneurial initiatives of the diaspora. It also recommended considering to foster tutorial programs to connect the diaspora with local entrepreneurs with complementary abilities and competence regarding the local markets. Finally, it suggested strengthening cooperation ties between companies in both origin and destination countries to support entrepreneurial initiatives of the diaspora in aspects such as knowledge exchange and technology transference by including innovative projects in national development policies and strategies. [2]

These recommendations make it evident to governments that it is necessary to design public policies to bond with their diaspora; and to pay close attention to their qualified diaspora. Evidently, there is no universal recipe; each country must identify its own advantages and find its own individual path. The idea underlying this is that each country must acknowledge its diaspora's capacities and innovation abilities, because these are today's most valuable development assets in the merging knowledge society.

In the last decades, three new tendencies of global qualified migration have become evident. It is mandatory to acknowledge them in order to identify the connection mechanisms of the qualified Mexican diaspora towards 2020: 1) The exponential growth of qualified migration [3], 2) A constant growth which surpasses medium and low qualified migration; and 3) The growing participation of qualified women migrants and the concentration of qualified human resources in developed countries (Lozano & Gandini, 2011). These tendencies are easily explained due to the fact that the most advanced economies have the largest innovation and scientific development centers which attract creative specialists generating knowledge in complex production processes.

The qualified Mexican diaspora

Even if there is no specific data, several sources confirm the growth of qualified Mexican migration. The most relevant of these present Mexico as the first exporter of highly qualified migration in Latin America and sixth worldwide, with 1.4 million professionals migrating toward OECD countries.

In the United States, for example, which is the number one destination country for qualified migration world-wide, the number of Mexicans with Bachelor's, Master's or Doctor's degrees grew 2.4 times between 2000 and 2012; that is, from 411 thousand to 1 million, 15 thousand people. From this total, 862 thousand (84.9%) has professional studies (Bachelor's, superior technician and/or Professional associate); the rest (153 thousand) have some postgraduate studies (15.1%). In other words, one in every 10 Mexicans with a professional degree and a little more than one in every four with postgraduate studies, live in the United States. [4]

For 2013, according to the American Community Survey (ACS), there are 160 thousand Mexicans with postgraduate studies living in the United States; 66.7 % of them have a Masters' degree, 24.3% have a professional degree and 9.0% have a Doctor's degree.

Other studies show that the number of highly qualified Mexican migrants is as high as two million. Numbers vary but we will consider the results of ACS and SELA (Latin American and Caribbean Economic System) on qualified migration towards OECD countries which highlights Mexico in Latin America with a major growth between 1990 and 2007 (270%). In 2007, the number reached was of 1'357,120 migrants.[5]

As we mentioned before, even considering the variations in the data, we are effectively speaking of almost one million and four hundred thousand qualified Mexican nationals living abroad. This fact, on its own, represents a fundamental economic resource for the creation of products, knowledge, technologies, ideas and creativity. By getting together to bond and organize themselves in order to support their country of origin, they are promoting change, innovation and openness towards the rest of the world.

The Mexican Model: The Network of Qualified Mexicans Abroad. "Mexican Global Network"

Mexico has made a very important progress in the direction of creating ties with its diaspora through the Institute for Mexicans abroad (IME). This entity, in the Ministry of Foreign Affairs, has created an innovative transnational model which aims to improve the living standards of the Mexican communities living abroad and their families living in Mexico.

One of the main strategies in this direction is the outreach and bonding with the highly qualified Mexican community abroad. This includes the possibility of building mechanisms in order to take advantage of the knowledge, experiences, contacts and relationships of this important group so as to overcome concepts like "brain drain" by promoting the ideas of "brain gain", "brain exchange" and "brain circulation". In other words, to view the Mexican qualified diaspora as a source of national and transnational development and networking.[6]

In this context, the Mexican Government set as a priority the creation of permanent communication programs with the qualified diaspora as well as the strengthening and consolidation of knowledge networks. The result is a model based on the paradigm of knowledge circulation so that talent and qualified mobility become an opportunity for national development and not a permanent loss of human resources. To do so, the Ministry of Foreign Affairs (through IME), CONACYT (the National Council for Science and Technology and FUMEC (the Mexico-United States Foundation for Science) since 2005, joined efforts to create the Talent Network of Mexicans Abroad.

When the Silicon Valley Chapter was constituted in California, USA, in 2006, the Network was formally created. Later its name was changed to: Mexican Global Network (*Red Global MX*). Its mission is for highly qualified Mexicans who live abroad and are linked to sectors or businesses of high added value contribute to support Mexico's insertion in the global economy, especially in what is called knowledge economy. A network of networks, an independent organization where highly qualified migrants interested in supporting Mexico, establish collaboration mechanisms with key Mexican institutions in strategic sectors.

IME has the support of Mexico's Embassies and Consulates in order to find and organize qualified Mexican nationals in each of their circumscriptions. They then organize themselves in geographical "chapters", define their goals and objectives and the mechanisms with which they will manage or govern their chapter. These chapters are groups with local identity which adhere to the Mexican Global Network or *"Red"* and, as organized civil societies, have a clear collaboration path and link with the Mexican Government to achieve the following goals:

To promote strong ties between Mexico and highly qualified Mexicans living abroad.

To favor Mexico's insertion in the global knowledge economy through the creation of links between this talent and its counterpart in Mexico.

To encourage the creation of high added value projects in areas such as business development, education for global innovation and support for Mexican communities abroad.

To foster a better understanding of the contributions of Mexicans abroad both in Mexico and in the countries where they currently live in.

To promote a prestigious image of México abroad.

In the past three years the network has received an unprecedented impulse by allowing the Mexican diaspora to bond, promoting capacities and knowledge from abroad, training human resources, supporting mentorships student and academic mobility, productive investments, scientific and cultural exchanges, the creation of new business and commercial ties, the exchange of experiences and contacts as well as philanthropic projects.

The main idea is to prevent Mexicans from losing contact with their country of birth. To do this, the *Network* has a Global Coordination and three regional ones (America, Europe, and Asia-Australia) which interact among themselves to create multinational projects. Representatives and directors of the different chapters get together in regional meetings which take place every year to develop a referential framework and strengthen each region and collaboration with the Mexican Global Network, IME, the network of Mexican Embassies and Consulates and other Mexican counterparts such as Conacyt, ProMéxico, Inadem, Anuies and Mexico's private academic sector.

These meetings also help to share better practices and successful projects as well as lessons learned in the past and to multiply profitable efforts in strategic areas for Mexico. This open dialogue has generated a better understanding of the current and potential roles of each chapter, and of the individuals which are part of them, in the context of the public diplomacy efforts of the Mexican diaspora.

As a result, since 2013, in an impact strategy towards 2020, to become a dynamic, autonomous self-sustained network of networks system, the *"Red"* (through its Global Coordination and its three regional coordination organizations), concentrates its liaison's efforts with Mexico in four central axes: Science, Academy and Technology, Business Entrepreneurship, Social Responsibility and Creative Industries and three strategic areas: knowledge transfer, innovation and self-sustained operation.

"Red Global MX" is, without any doubt, a transnational network which constitutes a key vehicle for knowledge to return to Mexico, a network of networks which has earned the rank of a world level ecosystem. In only two years it has multiplied its number of chapters from 21 in 2006 to 45 in 20 different countries and four continents in 2015. Currently, *"Red Global MX"*, is proud of an organized civil society of more than four thousand highly qualified Mexicans living abroad who are active in more than one hundred projects which aim to: contribute with a strategic approach in areas, technologies and global tendencies in their fields; support the promotion of Mexico's capacities to favor the market's new opportunities; promote strategic alliances; encourage the learning of better practices; facilitate knowledge transfer and the development of new abilities; generate mentorship for Mexican companies seeking international competiveness; foster business workshops and commercial missions; obtain mentorships for academic programs; encourage orientation for job abilities; stand up for professional practices and apprenticeships.

All these contributions allow Mexico to access different ecosystems which may launch capacities and businesses of high added value. They also allow talented people living in Mexico to be known and appreciated in such ecosystems. It is, undoubtedly, a successful program which is the result of a global consensus on the paramount role of migrants in their countries of origin as well as those of destination. Today international forums do not discuss the role of migrants. Instead, the mechanisms through which the equation migration-development can be optimized are the subject of these forums' analysis. In this new context, in which knowledge circulates, the talent of highly qualified migrants reaches an unprecedented multiplying potential which simultaneously and positively impact both in destination societies as well as in our country.

2020, a well-connected network of networks

Qualified Mexicans living abroad have successfully generated a unique transnational movement. Some of them have residence in two or three countries, they develop businesses and technologies in the most advanced worlds' economies, maintain a close bond with Mexico, and are happy to volunteer their time, expertise, contacts and knowledge. They constitute human capital willing to participate with the Mexican Government in the design of public policies in favor of innovation.

This will and capacity should flourish in the upcoming years to become a strategy that incorporates the Mexican diaspora in Mexico's migration public policies. By improving the existing organization model in which highly qualified Mexican migrants have a good communication and collaboration channel with the Mexican Government, we aim to impact in national development at all levels.

Today we know that our success is to have created the ideal mechanism to approach this important group of Mexican migrants. The following challenge is to envision this Network of networks as a liaison system between Mexico and its highly qualified diaspora so that, by 2020, a true talent circulation exists. To achieve this goal, public policies on migration together with national development strategies will create a solid innovation science and technology system to determine how to attract or retain talent bearing in mind the global competition for human capital.

It is very important to know where we are heading and how we can multiply the Network's outreach. According to some countries' experiences, networks should be divided vertically: by sector, industry or theme; and horizontally: according to their members' experience. This division allows participants to identify common interests so as to get involved with the networks...but there must be platforms in Mexico to channel this collaboration. In other words, there must be programs in Mexico which contemplate the organized qualified Mexican diaspora to help Mexico reach its maximum potential by summing the will of all Mexicans, including those living abroad.

An important element to take into consideration is reciprocity. Reciprocity is vital for the creation, growth and stability of the network. Members must receive tangible and intangible benefits for their participation. Benefits such as business opportunities or public acknowledgement for their support. Efficient talent networks must be more than social media or data bases; they must be organizations focused on generating results through specific activities and objectives. This is the challenge we have today. To be able to strengthen the network so that it gets the sufficient momentum to transcend by itself and to obtain positive results for everyone involved.

With all this in mind, by 2020 we will have a network with connection through an international and multidisciplinary platform of communication, consultancy, counseling and tutoring to guarantee global mobility for scientists, technologists and entrepreneurs. A systemized network with special directories able to place new networks, to actively participate in Mexico's innovation processes and, above all, to create a true interconnection in science, academy and technology to foster national abilities to compete internationally.

IME has already given a first step towards the goals for 2020: the liaisons with the private sector and organized civil society in Mexico through the creation of a figure called *"Nodos de la Red Global de Mexicanos Calificados en el Exterior"* (Nodes of the Mexican Global Network). These are Mexican organizations constituted at a local level which serve as development vehicles for local projects in Mexico. They have vast experience in technology innovation as well as entrepreneurship, coordination, execution and backup of different kinds of projects to foster technological development, joint design of patents and exchange of better practices. This mechanism is already delivering excellent results with a strong work relationship and proven dialogue with state governments.

Nodes promote the possibility for the qualified Mexican diaspora to articulate a network of national and international partners (academic institutions, research centers, businesses, industrial chambers, government secretaries, regional authorities, social organizations, etc.) in the development of regional/local projects; organization of conferences, forums, workshops, etc. which impact positively in state and region development efforts.

This initiative promotes positive communication and bonding of a great number of Mexicans working in new projects. Undoubtedly, the launching of the of *"Red Global MX's Nodos"* will be strategic to connect the network's chapters with its counterparts in Mexico. This, plus a transversal or inter-institutional correlation with other Mexican institutions such as Conacyt, Inadem,

ProMéxico and the Mexican Universities, will guarantee a substantial impact for the program's success.

With this path in mind, *"Red Global MX"* will become a reference for Mexican scientists, academics, entrepreneurs, businessmen, artists and students wishing to strengthen their bonds with Mexico and, at the same time, to deploy actions to increase their sense of belonging with their country of birth. The *"Red"* forces us to be creative since these transnational practices among qualified migrants are introducing new analysis elements for transnationalism. New questions arise regarding the role of international cooperation and multi-lateral organisms for the establishment of bridges for science and technology exchange. According to Portes: "transnationalism in professionals has the potential to significantly alter the scientific and technological knowledge in countries of origin" (Portes, 2007:36).[7]

A great challenge, in which IME is focusing, is precisely finding the right so that the *"Red"* attracts talent towards Mexico. One possibility is to incorporate foreign students, for which scholarship policies could constitute an important flow of qualified immigration. Mexico's large highly qualified diaspora provides many opportunities for internationalization. For this reason, the design of creative public policy solutions is paramount for effective talent circulation, to strengthen networks, and to generate platforms to foster better bonds with Mexico.

It is a fact that we must consider the sum of all these aspects in order to close the technological and innovation gap in Mexico. Actions such as Higher education exchanges are essential to promote an entrepreneurial culture which acknowledges the value of innovation as a source of international competitiveness and a better return for productive investments. For this reason our challenge is to maximize the strategic opportunity to attract Mexico's organized highly qualified diaspora through Mexican Global Network *"Red Global MX"*.

References

Bermudez, Rosa (2010) Migración calificada e integración en las sociedades de destino. Skilled migration and integration in host societies. CEDUA-. El Colegio de México Sociedad y Economía No. 19, pp. 135-150

Clemens, Michael (2010). "A labor mobility agenda for development". Working Paper 201, Washington DC: Center for Global Development. Disponible en: <http://ssrn.com/abstract=1543396> [Consulta: 25 de junio de 2010].

Clemens, Michael A. 2013. What Do We Know About Skilled Migration and Development? Washington, DC: Migration Policy Institute.

Coloma, Soledad. «Migración calificada en América Latina: similitudes y contras- tes». Andina Migrante, n° 13 (julio 2012): 2-14.

Cruz- Piñeiro, Rodolfo, Ruiz- Ochoa, Wilfrido, (2010). Migración calificada de mexicanos a Estados Unidos mediante visado preferencial, México, El Colegio de la Frontera Norte. CIEAP/UAEM.

Delgado-Wise, Raúl. Debate Migración mexicana altamente calificada: problemática y desafíos. Observatorio de Desarrollo, volumen 2, número 8.

Eighth Meeting of the Global Forum on Migration and Development 14-16 October 2015, Istanbul, Turkey. Sesión de Mesa redonda 3.2: Las alianzas entre el sector público y el privado para apoyar la iniciativa empresarial y la creación de empleo de los migrantes/la diáspora, con un enfoque sobre las pequeñas y medianas empresas. Disponible en http://www.gfmd.org/meetings/turkey2014-2015/rt-themes-and-govt-teams

Lozano, Fernado, Gandini, Luciana (2011) "Migración calificada y desarrollo humano en América Latina y el Caribe". Universidad Nacional Autónoma de México-Instituto de Investigaciones Sociales. Revista Mexicana de Sociología 73, núm. 4 (octubre-diciembre, 2011): 675-713. México, D.F. ISSN: 0188-2503/11/07304-05.

Pellegrino, Adela, (2001) Reflexiones sobre la Migración Calificada. Programa de Población de la Facultad de Ciencias Sociales de la Universidad de la República (Uruguay).

Tuirán, Rodolfo, Avila José Luis (2013) "Migración calificada entre México-Estados Unidos. Desafíos y opciones de política", México. Migración y Desarrollo Núm. 21- Segundo Semestre.

---

[1] Remittances were estimated at about USD 440 billion in 2014 (World Bank data). The diasporas' contributions may be grouped in direct foreign investment (DFI), commerce (including general and nostalgic) knowledge transference, return migration, trans-national entrepreneurial initiative and remittances.

[2] Migration World Forum –Round Table Session 3.2: Alliances between the public and private sectors to support entrepreneurial initiatives and the creation of Jobs for migrants/ the diaspora, focusing on small and médium businesses.

[3] Qualified migrants are those people who have completed the third or fourth level of studies (professional, graduate degrees) living in countries different from the country they were born in (SELA 2009; Lozano y Gandini 2011; Esteban 2011; Coloma 2012; Bermúdez 2012; Bermúdez 2014). They include different groups according to the reason of their qualified mobility: students, scientists, academics, executive workers, technicians, independent professionals, entrepreneurs, etc.

[4] Tuirán, Rodolfo, Ávila José Luis (2013) "Qualified migration between México and the United States. Challenges and policy options", México. Migration and Development Number 21- Second Semester.

[5] SELA: Sistema Económico Latinoamericano y del Caribe (2009)."Migration of qualified human resources from Latin-America and the Caribbean. Contemporary tendencies and perspectives"; Caracas, Venezuela.

[6] The qualified migration dynamics itself has fostered the idea, in countries of origin, that the so called loss or brain drain be transformed into a new idea of mobility of highly qualified agents to draw knowledge, scientific and technological development. On the other hand, countries of destination have implemented selectivity rules in migration policies favoring the reception of highly qualified migrants and making hiring more flexible.

[7] -Bermudez, Rosa (2010) Migración calificada e integración en las sociedades de destino. *Skilled migration and integration in host societies.* CEDUA-. El Colegio de México Sociedad y Economía No. 19, pp. 135-150 Disponible en http://www.scielo.org.co/scielo.php?script=sci_arttext&pid=S1657-63572010000200008

21

Extreme cultural landscapes in the context of globalisation: Mali, China and Mexico

PAMELA DURÁN DÍAZ, PH.D.*

*Postdoctoral fellow, lecturer and researcher in Ginna Kanda Research Group, Universitat Politècnica de Catalunya. Barcelona, Spain.

Globalisation and faltering economy are jeopardizing landscapes and forms of life that are world heritage, whether they have been recognized as such or not. In some cases, opening up to tourism is the best way to preserve a cultural landscape, while in other contexts, it is the fastest way to destroy it.

The relationship between cultural landscapes and development could be critical in both hypo and hyper-development contexts. In several cities in Europe, Asia, and America, tourist activities are an economic complement to consolidated commercial and industrial activities, however, in hypo-development cases, it may be the only option to prevent population displacements, with the consequential territory abandonment.

Several cultural landscapes declared World Heritage by UNESCO are already important tourist destinations; however, there is a latent lack of plans and studies to improve the quality of life of the inhabitants, who inherited an ancient culture that became tangible in their territory. On the other hand, there are many difficulties in obtaining information and mapping the land and its intangibles.

Culture is the fourth pillar of sustainable development, as Hawkes claimed over a decade ago. Keeping this idea in mind, we might understand cultural landscapes where both nature and men work together in perfect harmony. Those landscapes are extreme when located in places where the weather weak or rising economy (hypo/hyper-development) endangers unique, ancient ways of life.

In order to make a first approach to these countries we must recognize the multidimensionality of the concept of development, which could be cultural, economic, technological, or in human rights, among others. For instance, in Africa, there is a sense of time different from the Gregorian calendar, for centuries, this difference has been an argument to indicate a developmental impediment. In fact, several African civilizations do not conceive time as an incisive linear arrow but as a complex circular process, divided in the time of the dead, the time of the living and the time of those still unborn. This way of seeing time weaves it and makes it cyclic while it loads it of responsibility in relation to past and future generations. Interestingly, it is possible to compare this conception of time to sustainable development, which wields the banner of intergenerational equity, which means that extreme cultural landscapes are cherished by a cluster of intangible assets.

Those intangible assets are so fragile that even the actions to preserve the built heritage may infringe them. Therefore, new strategies should be traced, integrating intangible and built heritage, involving local people before setting intervention strategies in order to prevent the breach of the very sensitive identity. Therefore, identity should be considered in economic activation projects through urban planning strategies that promote cultural tourism.

With the criterion of *minimum intervention for maximum share*, the sustainable management of cultural tourism is an opportunity for development, as long as it is established as a form of exchange that considers both tangible and intangible expressions as an opportunity to highlight the uniqueness of the context.

Ginna Kanda International Forum for Sustainable Development of Extreme Cultural Landscapes is a research group of the Architecture School of Barcelona in Universitat Politècnica de Catalunya, which has been studying extreme cultural landscapes of Mali and China since 2005. From then on, several case studies have been considered (Mexico among them), as ideal sites for urban, architectural, landscape architecture, and academic projects for sustainable development in which the intangible assets become the engine for transformations, thereby improving the quality of life.

Cultural landscapes and the fragility of the intangibles

According to Sauer, *"a cultural landscape is transformed from a natural landscape by a local group. Culture is the agent, and the natural area is the medium. The cultural landscape is the result of that transformation"* (1925). Therefore, cultural landscapes are urban and regional locations where human action is displayed in the transformation of nature and the construction of unique landscapes full of history and contents. Through the recognition of the cultural value of landscapes from the identity, territorial projects include intangible assets as a mean of multidisciplinary, scientific, social and cultural approach, from understanding the complexity of such sites. Currently, few interventions that promote the transformation of the landscape consider local culture in a sense in which urban and economic development do not adversely affect the intangible assets.

Intangible assets are disembodied, ideal and abstract; they are actions that left their imprint on the site and on local architecture. The intangibles might not be seen, but the approach to other cultures is nurturing because of their presence.

Many hill tribes living around Sa Pa in Vietnam do not fear foreigners, because since the 18th Century, they got used to the passage of the French who settled a mountain station in the area. Until twenty years ago, economy based on agriculture, but the ban in opium[1] cultivation in Vietnam in 1993 caused a decrease of cash flow. Shortly afterwards, Sa Pa was rediscovered by European travelers. Thus locals, encouraged by economic reasons, have contributed to make it a thriving tourist destination.

While men work in the fields, women, in addition to housework, take care of everything else: they collect indigo, manufacture and dye fabrics, sew clothes, embroider, take care of animals [2], trade in Bac Ha weekly market and in various villages markets. In addition, women of various tribes of the Hmong ethnic group, whose language skills are admirable, serve as tourist guides to take travelers through the villages that hide at the edge of steep roads that coil along the mountain ridges and rice terraces. Although their written history has been lost on the road after centuries of emigration, the Hmongs have always carried with them their costumes and traditions. Until now. Until now that tourists invade their markets demanding souvenirs; or require spaces with electricity, drinking water and drainage to stay; or need motor vehicles to reach the high peaks of the mountain; or wear hiking shoes and waterproof jackets. Until now, when villages are being adapted to the comfort of others, local tribes begin to question whether their traditional way of life is the one they chose or the only one they knew so far.

Another case: for ethnic groups living in Prey Lang, the "forest of spirits" in Cambodia, tourism is the least of the harms that stalk them, as the government has authorized the progressive destruction of the woods on behalf of logging companies, rubber plantations and mining companies. To evaluate the possibility of preserving the forest as a nature reserve with tourist routes, it should be understood that tourism itself is not the solution, but it is a way to start the economic engine; which means that the installation of touristic infrastructure could be motivated by a cultural rather than economic exchange. Meanwhile, the establishment of large industries in the area has expelled the natives, their spirits and one of the most sustainable cyclic plantation systems known to humankind. Even with the idea of *minimum intervention for maximum share* (Ginna Kanda's motto), it is difficult to adapt the entrance into the woods for tourism without violating the intangibles, since access is conditioned to the permission of the forest spirits. However, as the intangible assets have religious roots that have already been secularized, nature predominates as a hint of the intangible.

How to prevent the destruction of reality on behalf of creating scenery for tourists? "The rescue of endangered cultural landscapes should be done in compliance with local beliefs, since the commitment to local culture has an impact in society", says Malian architect Mamadou Koné. Koné, with the support of UNESCO, has been in charge of preserving the built heritage in Néni and Mori, sometimes restoring temples in which their status as sacred places imposed difficulties such as working barefoot, without artificial light, and performing rituals in order to sanctify places that had been touched. The value of vernacular architecture is not only in that its form and materials are functional concerning to local livelihood systems, but also most of its value is intangible. The restoration of those temples with outside techniques with no regard for the indigenous beliefs would have made the sacred places lose their authenticity in exchange for freezing a moment in time. Thus, locals would not feel any ties with the restored temples, making them become scenery for tourists. In the cultural landscape, architecture ceases to be a built environment in order to become a material cultural element.

Building a method to manage extreme cultural landscapes

Ginna Kanda has been working on practical applications of the theoretical studies developed so far. The aim is to create a methodology of territorial representation and interpretation of the landscape and built heritage of case studies in different contexts, while intangible heritage is studied in order to trace intervention strategies that would promote sustainable development. For the extrapolation of the methodology, it is important that the case studies do not follow the same pattern, therefore, they should be placed in different countries, have a variety of sizes, scale approaches, levels of development, biophysical conditions, ecosystems, traditions, and cultures.

Among the immense possibilities, three case studies have been selected for building the method: China, Mali and Mexico, representing hyper-development, hypo-development and a bridge between the previous two, respectively. The methodology to study the built and intangible heritage of the named case studies involves the construction of maps showing landscape elements, the spatial configuration of the territory, territorial dynamics, identifying structuring elements and identifying the intangible assets.

Beijing, in China, is a city whose growing economy and openness to globalization has generated an accelerated development with its consequent identity crisis. There are more than 4.500 streets that conform the *hutong*[3] in potential risk of progressive destruction since Beijing Olympic Games in 2008. Due to their centric location, the land value makes the urban layout and the traditional architecture prone to be replaced by new housing and new monuments to modern architecture [4]. In addition, the series of seven concentric rings that form the basis of Beijing's urban morphology has gradually spread on agricultural lands, causing both the disappearance of labor fields to feed the city's population, and the exodus of farmers to the urban area. About 70% of the people who use the public transportation system in Beijing are farmers who have been forced to move to the city in search for work. This is an unsustainable model that involves the loss of intangible values and local identity, as the millenary identity is compromised by accelerated development. This phenomenon, present in the Republic's capital city, is a large-scale reflection of what happens in the different inner provinces, such as Huangtupo and Badong counties in Hubei province, by Yagtze river, comprising a complex territory of an extension of more than 6 km whose population has been evacuated due to the flooding of the Three Gorges Dam. The new towns built to house the displaced population are large-size, low-quality containers at a permanent risk of landslides, while the ancient villages that contain the history of the region stand as enormous empty skeletons.

On the other hand, ancestral forms of life present in Bandiagara Cliff in Dogon Country (Mali) have been affected since its declaration as World Heritage Site by UNESCO in 1989. Although the restoration of built monuments have been successful from the architectural point of view, which should have had a positive impact on the social cohesion and the economy of one of the ten poorest countries in the world[5], has resulted in the loss of intangible assets due to lack of identity elements in the intervention projects. For instance, the restoration of the Great Mosque of Djenne, which respected the façade and original layout, and mixed traditional architecture with modern building techniques and materials, at the time it led to a temporary economic mobilization concentrated in the area. However, in the long run, the impact has not been as positive as expected: the restoration of the mosque with local materials (such as clay, straw, and natural binders) involved an annual pilgrimage, thus, the activation of local economy through the exchange and collaboration of several villages. The restoration with imported weatherproof materials (such as concrete or clay mixed with cement as binder) formed, on one hand, the loss of the annual festival to rebuild the mosque, and on the other, the alteration of the intangible values by not respecting the ancestral standards for building procedures for sacred places. Djenne mosque is just one of many examples in Mali of the effect of the ignorance of local culture by visitors, even when involving good intentions.

Across the world, intangibles abound in Mexican culture, from the traditional festivals, food, music, language (derived from a mixture of Castilian with local indigenous dialects). For instance, the Great Pyramid of Cholula, Tlachihualtépetl (the "handmade hill" in Nahuatl) is disguised as a prominent hill topped by the Sanctuary of la Virgen de los Remedios. The 2300-year-old archaeological site comprises a series of layers of the different civilizations that occupied the site since pre-Hispanic times until the Spanish Conquest. Being through history one of the most important ceremonial centers in Mexico, the Great Pyramid of Cholula is strongly linked to the identity of the region. Also, rural land for flower plantations around the pyramid, while enhancing such identity, acts as a buffer for urban growth. Though, recent government initiatives plan to transform the surroundings of the archaeological site into a commercial and tourist pole of growth, meaning the expropriation of protected and rural land for shopping, parking and advertisement. Therefore, the fact that the site has been active since its construction until today, has been on one hand, its greatest achievement, and, on the other hand, its greatest threatening. Due to shared historic and current conditions of threats in a global world where economic development is a priority, Mexico could act as a bridge between Europe, Africa and Asia, and could serve both as a reference and as a lab for the implementation of sustainable development criteria.

At present, the recognition of intangible assets for interventions in the territory is limited and fairly recent, since the introduction of the concept of Intangible Cultural Heritage in 2003, UNESCO makes an effort to identify and preserve these intangible assets. The need for reconnaissance surveys of the built and intangible heritage was originated by the search for a new management model for cultural tourism that, rather than pausing a site in time for touristic contemplation, conducts the preservation of traditions and their natural evolution through exchange.

Regardless of the initially selected case studies, the purpose of Ginna Kanda is to implement the study of endangered cultural landscapes while mapping the intangibles. As a part of the practical research, diagnoses are carried out through the construction of a dynamic cartography that should show the traces of the historic city, the transformations of the urban artefact, and the permanence and/or disappearance of the intangible elements of the local culture, in order to develop interventional strategies. The utility of this research would be the applicability of the methodology in practically any given case study. The participation of international students, researchers and fellows is highly encouraged, promoting the inclusion of the academic and professional community with local authorities and citizens, which would raise the awareness regarding the intangible assets and sustainable development.

The role of UNESCO in the preservation of built and intangible heritage

Since the actions of UNESCO to preserve the archaeological and historical temples of Abu Simbel in

Egypt in 1959 until now, more than one thousand sites around the world have been entitled as World Heritage. However, in view of the tendency to cultural homogenization due to the effects of globalization, UNESCO officially introduced in 2003 the definition of Intangible Cultural Heritage as the following.

"The intangible cultural heritage means the practices, representations, expressions, knowledge, skills-as well as the instruments, objects, artefacts and cultural spaces associated therewith-that communities, groups and, in some cases, individuals recognize as part of their cultural heritage. This intangible cultural heritage, transmitted from generation to generation, is constantly recreated by communities and groups in response to their environment, their interaction with nature and their history, and provides them with a sense of identity and continuity, thus promoting respect for cultural diversity and human creativity. For the purposes of this Convention, consideration will be given solely to such intangible cultural heritage as is compatible with existing international human rights instruments, as well as with the requirements of mutual respect among communities, groups and individuals, and of sustainable development" (UNESCO, 2003).

In Mali, UNESCO has recognized as World Heritage the ancient cities of Djenne (1988), the ancient city of Timbuktu (1988), the tomb of Askia (2004) and Bandiagara Cliff in Dogon Country (1989). From this recognition, several action plans for the preservation of architectural heritage have been set. But, in the case of Bandiagara Cliff –Ginna Kanda's case study-, we are not talking about a large city's old town or a small village, but an extension of 400.000 hectares which includes 289 villages with different ecosystems. It is a vulnerable area on a number of fronts: climate change, tourism, time and economy. Thus, scarcity pushes the abandonment of a traditional way of life intimately linked to the landscape and the territory from the social, cultural and economic points of view, favoring tourist development as the income of external resources.

According to UNESCO, the territory of Bandiagara Cliff is listed a National Heritage of Mali by Decree 89-428 P-RM of 28th of December 1989 as natural and cultural sanctuary. There are also valid laws as the forestry exploitation law 68-8/AN-RN of February 1968, and the hunting ordinance 60/CMLN of the 11th of November 1969. The Ministry of Culture of Mali (who bears the responsibility of protecting this territory) has delegated the management of Bandiagara Cliff to the Cultural Mission of Bandiagara. They prepared a land management and preservation plan for 2006-2010, where the implementation of programs related to preservation was required, with the intention of improving living conditions of the inhabitants –the true heirs of the heritage assets of the site.

In China, UNESCO has declared as World Heritage 33 architectural assets since 1987 until 2014 (besides of 10 natural parks and 4 mixed sites). Among them, the site of Peking Man in Zhukudian (1987), the Imperial Palaces of Ming and Qing dynasties in Beijing and Shenyang (1987), the Temple of Heaven (1998), the Summer Palace and Imperial Garden in Beijing (1998), the Imperial Tombs of Ming and Qing dynasties (2000), the Great Canal (2014) and the Great Wall (1987). The laws that protect Cultural Relics in China and the regulations on the management of cultural heritage sites, managed by the State

Administration of Cultural Heritage, provide legal, institutional and administrative guarantees to ensure the maximum protection of the authenticity and integrity of the heritage site. However, intensive tourism and urban hyper-development of large cities (Beijing specifically) have a negative impact both in recognized heritage areas and in those that have not been yet recognized by UNESCO. For instance, the damage suffered by architectural monuments such as the Imperial Palaces of the Forbidden City, produced by intensive tourism exploitation. Also, the *hutongs*, the alleys of old Beijing built during the Yuan, Ming and Qing dynasties, have been progressively demolished to make way for modern development. It is important to note that both initiatives (the intensive tourism and the demolition of the *hutongs*) were carried out by the City of Beijing Administration.

Moreover, Mexico has 32 cultural, natural and mixed sites recognized by UNESCO, from the pre-Hispanic city of Teotihuacan (1987) to the Central Campus of Universidad Nacional Autónoma de México (2007); plus 8 registries in the List of Intangible Cultural Heritage, including pre-Hispanic festivals dedicated to the commemoration of the dead (2008), the ritual ceremony of Voladores de Papantla (2009), traditional Mexican cuisine (2010), Mariachi (2011), and the Centre for the Totonaca Indian Arts (2012). The National Institute of Anthropology and History (INAH) guards the archaeological sites recognized by UNESCO. Also, there is the Federal Law on Monuments and Archaeological, Artistic and Historical Sites, in force since 1972.

UNESCO has legislative scopes worldwide, which imply introducing economic resources for the preservation of the sites and the opening of such site for tourist uses.

However, these advantages may also be the greatest weaknesses of UNESCO's method, as the protected elements are usually preserved to face tourists while turning its back to the locals. Thus, while the built heritage is protected, the lack of understanding towards the intangible cultural values causes the cultural isolation of the protected element. As a result, the community no longer feels identified with it and is excluded from the preservation process.

Even though the cultural value of the knowledge and practices related to *imzad* in the Taureg communities (in Algeria, Mali and Niger) was recognized in 2013, to date, the lifestyle, the ritual masks, the graves, or the Dogon traditional routes (to name a few in Bandiagara Cliff) have not been recognized. About China, UNESCO has an extensive list of cultural intangible heritage, including the crafts linked to traditional architecture with wood frames, traditional designs and construction techniques with wooden arch bridges (2009). China has faced countless internal struggles in which the territory has expanded, contracted, broken, and restored many times, while grouping different ethnicities and customs in an area of almost 10 million km². However, we must understand that Chinese civilization has had, from the Xia Dynasty (c. 2000 BC) until the 20th Century, few outside influences; therefore, it is a unique case study in which it is possible to observe the sociocultural evolution of civilization in an almost continuous line. Though, the introduction of economic reforms in 1978 led to the fastest economic growth worldwide, and to the opening to globalization that involves an identity crisis with its consequent loss of traditions and intangible assets. The urban effects of this phenomenon is the devaluation of the *hutong* in favor of modern business and housing complexes that reproduce

European aesthetics without consideration of the local traditions (as in Tianducheng, Shanghai, built in 2007 as a copy of Paris). As a result, they end up being ghost towns. From the economic point of view, the loss of identity is manifested in the replica and reproduction of foreign goods, damaging productive creativity.

Ginna Kanda as a catalyzer for development

Following the implementations of the plan drawn by UNESCO, Ginna Kanda has recognized the lack of information, and detected the need of studying territories within the frame of cultural landscapes in the fields of land planning, landscape, architecture and land management. The purpose is that, applying the tools we have as professionals and researchers, we could interpret the results in order to search for local collaboration, resulting in the transformation of cultural landscapes into engines of sustainable development to benefit local communities.

Ginna Kanda has generated collaborative links with academic and research purposes with prestigious international universities, such as Universitat Politècnica de Catalunya (Spain), Ecole Superieur d'Ingenierie, d'Architecture et d'Urbanisme de Bamako (Mali), Tsinghua University (China) and China University of Geosciences, in order to allow international exchanges of students between Europe, Africa and Asia. The consolidation of new links in Mexico, Latin America and the United States of America is in progress.

So far, three specialization courses for Mali have been carried out with students of architecture from Bamako and Barcelona. As a result, we have generated an updated cartography of Bandiagara Cliff, from satellite images and field trips, including the intangible assets, from which several landscape intervention projects were developed proposing tangible elements to interpret and explain the features of local identity to the visitors –the cultural tourists- in order to sensitize them.

In China, six workshops have been conducted since 2007. There, students from Barcelona and China were in charge of recognizing the intangible elements of the collective memory and the culture in sites as challenging as Huangtupo, Badong and Panjiayuan Market. Then, strategic projects were traced.

In Mexico, an updated cartography of Ciudad Victoria has been built, being the first morphogenetic atlas of the territory, with strategies for San Marcos river that have been considered for the urban development plan. Cholula's cartography has also been updated in order to study the pattern of land use and to identify the stakeholders, which lead to the definition of a spatial development strategy involving sociocracy. Ginna Kanda seeks for sponsors as CONACyT, La Caixa Bank, Banco Santander, and collaborative partners as Universidad Autónoma de Tamaulipas, Instituto Tecnológico y de Estudios Superiores de Monterrey, Universidad de las Américas Puebla and Universidad La Salle. Meanwhile, the theory behind the territorial dialectics and the identity has been an essential part of the debate in the workshops in Spain, China and Mali.

The educational project implies a new social consideration of the landscape as a cultural asset of remarkable value, and involves the diagnosis of the current situation in which the heritage value is threatened by urban development, and the awareness of the scientific community and students of architecture, who in the near future will spearhead the protection or destruction of built and intangible heritage.

The theoretical axis of the educational project is: 1) the recognition of the built heritage by UNESCO; 2) the cartography building process and territorial diagnose by Ginna Kanda; 3) the design of intervention strategies via urban, architectural and landscape projects by professionals and students in international workshops.

To do so, besides of using the appropriate software for drafting, mapping and updating the cartography of the territory, the use of satellite images is complemented with field trips. Site visits have the aim of making a photographic record of the site while searching for cultural exchange. Through the host/guest experience, the contact with foreigners allows the recognition, the approach, the awareness, and the verbal and written explanation of the landscape and the intangibles.

While UNESCO recognizes the value of tangible assets, Ginna Kanda distinguishes the intangible heritage that has not been mapped before. Therefore, the sum of these two criteria is a great opportunity for developing integrated projects that could be included in local legislations and in regional development plans.

Visioning extreme cultural landscapes towards 2025

The sustainable management of cultural landscapes is an opportunity for development, as long as it is established as a form of exchange to consider the tangible and intangible elements of the local culture. Whenever economic development involves the inclusion of cultural tourism, it should not be invasive, nor it should pretend to freeze in time reminiscences of the past, but it should contribute to preserve a living culture, immerse in an unstoppable evolutionary process. Interventions should be done respecting local traditions with a vision of development in which the exchange brought by tourism could increase the quality of life and bring economic benefits for local population.

A key strategy consists of the survey and diagnosis of the territory, through recognition and analysis studies. This phase of sustainable development must include social participation (locals, administratives, academics) in the tracing of strategic projects that would contribute to the sensitization and the recognition of local identity.

Another strategy is to prepare tourism and tertiary infrastructure strongly based on identity, memory, and collective imaginary. This would open the doors to a sensitive and respectful visitor, while activating the economy, the preservation of the built heritage, the recognition of intangible values, and cultural exchange.

However, the limitations of the problem are often economic: there are ancestral ways of life about to disappear due to the lack of resources, or because they are being engulfed by urban development. In government action plans, economy is usually a priority, before sustainability and cultural preservation.

Also, globalization acts as an economic and cultural homogenizer, with paradoxical effects in which fair trade actions are taking place, while the economic gap is increasingly evident at all levels of development. With this in mind, let us take a second look at our case studies. China is developing at the expense of their human and natural resources, with political actions that ignore international agreements in terms of environmental sustainability, working conditions and life quality. On the other hand, Mexico has serious socio-political and economic problems, due to insecurity, corruption and impunity, aggravated by the war against drug dealing. In the same line, the recent attacks in Burkina Faso and Mali by militant groups affiliated to Al-Qaeda and Islamic State has weakened West Africa in terms of security, quality of life, and economy. The relegation of the preservation of cultural landscapes to the background is unavoidable. It is inevitable to recall the destruction of the 1700-year-old statues of Buddha by the Taliban in the Bamiyan Valley of Afghanistan in 2001.

Thus, the future of urban planning of extreme cultural landscapes in the context of globalization is twofold. The first possibility: in view of the limited resources and lack of interest, many ancient cultural landscapes, together with their intangible values, will be progressively destroyed and occupied by a rather modern global urban culture, with the consequential increased poverty through the consumption of rural and natural lands. In a glimpse, it is possible to see that Africa is currently an immense lab where drones are being tested, which would lead to new urban planning strategies in terms of infrastructures. The risk involved in such measures without awareness of the importance of cultural landscapes, would be the destruction of natural and cultural heritage to give way to large containers. Connectivity would be subject to goods trading rather than human interaction. In a context in which people have more access to internet than to drinking water, the threat of this future is imminent.

The other possibility, however, is more promising. The future of urban planning points towards the design of smart cities, hence, the opportunity to humanize cities, making them more environmentally friendly, more accessible, more efficient in terms of transportation and metabolism, makes us think that it is possible to believe that, in the city of the near future, intangible values will also be recognized. Cultural tourism is one of the many alternatives to prevent the destruction of cultural landscapes without disrupting the intangibles, as long as the resulting economic growth improves the quality of life of the community instead of transforming traditional ways of life into servitude and entertainment for tourists.

Ginna Kanda has been taking actions in terms of generating knowledge through the construction of a dynamic methodology, the survey and mapping of the studied territories and their intangibles, and, equally important, sensitizing the community through scientific dissemination, cultural exchange and teaching. When those actions have a domino effect in other research groups, communities and administrations, many cultural landscapes would be recognized, reversing the negative effects of globalization (such as the loss of identity) without undermining the positive effects in terms of economy, openness to the world, access to information and technology, and social equality.

Whether pessimistic or hopeful, the destruction of many cultural landscapes is unfortunately unavoidable, since the awareness of their importance is not yet widely disseminated. In 2025, countless landscapes will be irrevocably destroyed or damaged. Nevertheless, there will be a new generation of professionals, already aware, already sensitive, who will not be as flexible as we are today towards sustainable development. Such lack of flexibility will not be given by stiffness, but by the impossibility of taking actions different from trying to reverse the damage previous generations made, due to their (our) lack of transgenerational vision. A vision that, it must be said, has been present in societies not as modern as Western civilization.

Cultural landscapes should –and someday will– be considered as catalyzers for transformation and social unity, because of their strong bonds with local identity. In places where there is no room for modernity, the recognition of intangible values do fit, as well as the respect towards their evolutionary time and space.

References

BARCELÓ, M. Quaderns d'Africa. Galaxia Gutenberg. Barcelona, 2004.

BEUADOIN, G. Les Dogons du Mali. BDT, Developpement, Paris, 1997.

CLEMENTI, A. Interpretazioni di paesaggio Convenzione Europea e innovazioni di método a cura di. Roma, 2002.

COUNCIL OF EUROPE. European landscape convention. Firenze, 2000.

CULTURES DEL MON. Arte en el País Dogón. Ajuntament de Palma, 1994.

DE BENOIST, R. Le Mali. L'Harmattan, Paris, 1998.

DIKEC, M. Badlands of the Republic, Space, Politics and Urban Politicy. Blackwell Publishing, Oxford, 2007.

DURÁN DÍAZ, P. Urbanismo sostenible y desarrollo, ¿una utopía? Barcelona-Ciudad Victoria. Master Degree Thesis. Departament d'Urbanisme i Ordenació del Territori. Universitat Politècnica de Catalunya. Barcelona, 2009.

DURÁN DÍAZ, P. El río como eje de vertebración territorial y urbana. El río San Marcos en Ciudad Victoria, México. Doctoral Thesis. Departament d'Urbanisme i Ordenació del Territori. Universitat Politècnica de Catalunya. Barcelona, 2014.

GRIAULE, M. Dios de Agua. Ad Litteram, Alta Fulla. Barcelona, 2000.

HAWKES, J. The fouth pillar of sustainability. Culture's essential role in public planning. Cultural Development Network, City of Melbourne, 2001.

HUET, J.C. Villages perchés des dogons du Mali. L'Harmattan, París, 1994.

KRONENBURG, R. Flexible, arquitectura que integra el cambio. Art Blume, Barcelona, 2007.

LLOP, C.; SABATÉ, J.; VILANOVA, J.M. Dels llocs memorables als paisatges culturals. Barcelona, COAC, 2003.

REVISTA ALTAÏR. Caminos de Tombuctú. Num. 11. Barcelona, 1991.

ROGER, A. Breu tractat del paisatge. Obertures (La Campana); 8. Barcelona La Campana, 2000.

UNESCO. Convención para la protección del patrimonio cultural y natural. Organización de las Naciones Unidas para la Educación, la Ciencia y la Cultura. París, UNESCO, 1972.

GAMBINI, R. Piani paesistici. Uno sguardo s'insieme en Urbanistica, no. 90, 1998.

Scientifica. Romma, 1994.

PRATS, LL. Antropología y patrimonio. Barcelona, Ariel, 1997.

SAUER, C. The morphology of landscape. University of California Publications in Geography 2: 19-54, 1925.

SCHUMACHER, M.; Peri-urban development in Cholula Mexico: towards a socio-spatial management model. Doctoral Thesis. Lehrstuhl für Bodenordnung und Landentwicklung. Technische Universität München. Munich, 2016.

UNESCO. Text of the Convention for the Safeguarding of the Intangible Cultural Heritage. General Conference in Paris, from 29th September to 17th October 2003.

UNESCO. Cultural landscapes:

http://www.unesco.org/culture/ich/index.php?lg=es&pg=00011

http://whc.unesco.org/exhibits/cultland/landscap.htm

http://whc.unesco.org

nwhc.fr/pages/home/pages/homepage.htm

---

[1] Or rather, the cultivation of opium poppy, the "flower of opium."

[2] For hill tribes, animals are part of marriage arrangements.

[3] Hutong: term of Mongolian origin meaning "water well", which since the 15th Century refers to the residential quarter surrounding the Forbidden City.

[4] Such as the headquarters of China Central Television CCTV by Rem Koolhaas, and the temple of consumption Galaxy Soho by laureate architect Zaha Hadid, both in the nearby Beijing Central Business District.

[5] According to the World Bank Group and the United Nations.

22

Planet-measuring shadows, Big Science, and new minds

Scattered thoughts on the future of experimental science

LUIS ROBERTO FLORES CASTILLO, PH.D.*

*Assistant Professor, Department of Physics, The Chinese University of Hong Kong; Scientific Research Prize 2012 of the Mexican Physics Society; member of the team that discovered the Higgs Boson, CERN, Switzerland.

The surprising pace of technological change has had a very significant impact on the natural sciences. The recent past offers some rather spectacular examples, with implications that we are yet to understand fully, but which importance would be difficult to overestimate.

The adoption of ever faster and cheaper tools to produce and analyze massive amounts of data, and the growing size of scientific collaborations made possible by new communication and collaboration technologies, have recently brought about several paramount scientific breakthroughs. Just to set the stage, let's take a quick look at three of them:

The full sequencing of the human genome, thanks to which it is already possible today to have your own genome sequenced and find out whether you are at risk of developing a number of significant health conditions. Furthermore, it is also already possible to alter the genetic makeup of organisms, with far-reaching ethical and legal implications.

The discovery of the Higgs boson. The ability to generate hundreds of millions of particle collisions *per second*, store a fraction of them in computing centers all over the world, and analyze overnight the petabytes of data accumulated during years of operation, allowed the discovery of this particle, which confirmed the existence of an all-encompassing object (the "Higgs field") intimately related to the origin of mass, and hence to the existence of atoms and to the behavior of matter.

The discovery of Dark Energy. The ability to gather *every night* data from *hundreds of thousands* of galaxies allowed astronomers to analyze in detail the rate of expansion of the universe, and to establish the fact that, contrary to all previous expectations, such expansion proceeds at an *ever increasing rate*. Very little is understood yet about the mechanism that causes this, but it radically changes our understanding of the large-scale behavior and structure of the universe, and of its possible ultimate fate.

New technologies and tools are likely to enable even farther-reaching breakthroughs in the next few decades. One paramount example is the development of non-invasive brain scanning technologies that already make it possible to determine the connection pathways between brain regions, and even neuron-level activation patterns with a time-resolution of *milliseconds*. In other words, we can already obtain a map of brain connections and even take a video of how and when *individual neurons* are activated.

Much more can be said about each of these and other topics; but for now let's just use the above as illustration of the impact that technological change has brought about.

The goal of this chapter is to provide a **very** brief look at foreseeable developments in the field of particle physics. The choice of topics is rather arbitrary, and necessarily limited, but it intends to work as a teaser for the reader. We will proceed in three sections: the first one aims to illustrate the power of the tools in use today; the second one describes some of the large-scale projects currently under study, and the third one intends to look further into the future, with the goal of enticing the imagination rather than to attempt any sort of forecasting.

From Eratosthenes to the Higgs boson

It goes without saying that new technologies enable new ways to explore Nature's mechanisms; however, with the rapid pace of tool development in many fields, it is often difficult to keep up with how far things *already are* today. Since we aim to have a brief look at some future possibilities, and what they may imply, we need to remind ourselves, even if briefly, of the state-of-the-art of experimental capabilities, and what it has made possible. What instruments, ideas and tools are available today to probe the nature of what we now call "fundamental interactions" and how far have they taken us already?

Rather than merely listing some of these capabilities, let me try to illustrate how these tools have extended our reach to probe into Nature by looking back to a relatively well-known example of experimental science, from around 200 BC. At the time, Eratosthenes of Cyrene, Chief Librarian at the Library of Alexandria, learned about an interesting curiosity: every year, at noon on the day of the summer solstice, vertical structures in the city of Syene produced no shadow; i.e., the Sun was exactly in the Zenith. Living in Alexandria, he was aware that, at noon on the same day, poles and buildings did produce a small but definite shadow in his city. Using little more than these simple facts, some basic geometry, and a measurement of the distance between the two cities, he was able to determine nothing less than *the size of Earth*. His tools? Little more than pen and paper. From such a meager bag of experimental tools and inputs, he managed to successfully *measure the size of a planet*.

Let's now fast-forward to our time, and very briefly tally the tools at our disposal. After two thousand years creating and refining models, tools and instruments, how do our tools compare with his? and how much further have they taken us? the discovery of the Higgs boson, briefly referred to at the beginning of this chapter, provides a rather illustrative example of some of the tools currently used at the forefront of Experimental Physics. These tools are often, justifiably, left out of descriptions of the discovery; to illustrate their reach and variety, I'll limit myself to only three examples here:

An effective collaboration among thousands of researchers. Together, the ATLAS and CMS experimental collaborations comprise about *six thousand* researchers stationed all over the world; collaborative actions of such large teams can only be accomplished timely through heavy use of effective communication technologies. During the months and weeks leading to the discovery, a large number of virtual meetings were needed, gathering researchers from all over the world in a non-stop round-the-clock effort.

The construction and operation of the largest scientific instrument in history –the Large Hadron Collider, a particle collider spanning a 27-kilometer circumference, buried a hundred meters below ground.

The organized and effective use of over 250 thousand computing cores distributed in about 170 computing centers in over thirty countries, and

The detailed theoretical modeling and analysis of the *tens of millions of millions* of particle collisions gathered over a two-year period. This modeling involved the use of state-of-the-art mathematical and computing tools.

Comparing these numbers with the single-man three-measurements effort that Eratosthenes carried out, there is, indeed, quite a large increase in the resources used; how do the results compare? from those very scarce inputs, he managed to *measure a planet...* what do we have to show for our much larger investment?

Interestingly, there is a sense in which the discovery of the Higgs boson is analogous to what Eratosthenes achieved. At the time, not much was known about the large-scale structure of the universe, and a determination of the size of the planet probed the properties of one of the largest objects known to man back then. Since then, much has been learned about the size and structure of the universe, and we know of objects much, much larger than our planet. The diameter of the sun, for example, is about a hundred times larger than Earth's, and there are stars hundreds of times larger than our sun. Our galaxy, the Milky Way, is a *million million* times larger than our sun, and it is only one of about *one hundred billion galaxies* in the visible universe. The universe itself is estimated to be about a hundred billion light-years across, which means that our planet, as large and majestic as it appears to us, is still an insignificant spot in such an immensity; the diameter of the (known) universe is about *a hundred million million million* times larger than that of our dear planet Earth.

And yet, besides galaxies, stars, planets, rocks, dust and radiation, we now know that all that immensity is also filled by an additional object, which we call the *Higgs field*. Without this extra component, the basic constituents of matter and forces would be unable to form atoms, solid objects, planets, stars ... and life. This object fills *all of space*, it has been present from the beginning of time, and will last until the end of the universe. It covers all regions of space from here to the farthest galaxy, and its action is also crucial in the smallest of regions, like the space between the nucleus of every atom and its electrons. This field is the largest single physical object that can possibly exist in our universe, and we have confirmed its existence precisely thanks to this massive worldwide investment in infrastructure, operation and data analysis. Following on Eratosthenes footsteps, we have managed to use curiosity, experiment, and math to extract information about the large-scale structure of our universe.

The near future

The discovery of the Higgs boson constituted an important success for Particle Physics and, rather soon, it pointed the way for future developments. Besides its existence, the very first piece of information that we were able to learn from the discovery was the mass of the new particle, and this is already modifying significantly the future possibilities for the field of high-energy physics.

The Large Hadron Collider, upgraded to a much larger collision rate (hence called the *High Luminosity LHC*), is expected to continue in operation as the world's most powerful accelerator until around 2035. However, given the size, cost and complexity of this type of very large instruments, long before the Higgs discovery particle physicists started discussing what type of experimental facility to build next. Without any experimental guidance (e.g., the discovery of a new particle, a new phenomenon, or a clear discrepancy between theory and experimental measurements), the "best" collision energy for a new particle accelerator was anybody's guess. Many agreed that the best strategy was to push the center-of-mass energy as high as possible, which implied aiming for the construction of linear colliders instead of circular colliders because, at very high energies, circular colliders loose a prohibitive fraction of their energy to radiation. Linear colliders do not have this problem, but some of the technologies needed to build them are still under development.

However, this scenario changed radically once the Higgs particle was discovered. The mass of the Higgs boson turned out to be relatively small. With such a "low" value, the construction of a circular collider tuned for massive production of Higgs bosons (hence named a "Higgs-factory") suddenly became a very attractive alternative. Instead of linear colliders aimed at much higher energies (to look for unknown new particles), the new collider would accelerate electrons versus their anti-particles (positrons), with a center-of-mass energy of precisely twice the mass of the Higgs boson; why that value?

Because operating at that energy, this machine would produce *millions* of Higgs boson pairs in a few years, hence providing an exceptional opportunity to study in detail the Higgs field and its interactions with all other fields. Moreover, after a few years of operation, such an accelerator can be dismantled, and the circular tunnel and infrastructure that hosts it can be reused for a new collider, which would use much more energetic projectiles instead of electrons and positrons.

At the time of this writing (early 2016) there are two independent large-scale efforts preparing proposals for such circular machines. Both proposals would dwarf the 27-kilometer Large Hadron Collider. One of them, so far named the *Future Circular Collider* (FCC), would be hosted at CERN and aims to build an accelerator of 80 or 100 kilometers in circumference. The second one has been called the *Circular Electron Positron Collider* (CEPC); its circumference would be between 50 and 100 kilometers and it would be hosted by China. Both proposals contemplate a second phase of operation. After a number of years of electron-positron collisions, much more energetic proton-proton collisions would start, with an energy significantly above that of the LHC.

To illustrate the difference, let's look at a couple of numbers. One of the many unintuitive predictions of the Special Theory of Relativity that have been thoroughly confirmed, is the following: when an object moves, its mass increases. It happens to all objects, but for those in our daily experience the effect is tiny. Even a 1-ton satellite, orbiting Earth at 14 thousand km/h, would increase its mass by barely one ten-thousandth *of a gram*. At the LHC, the speed of each proton is so close to the speed of light that the corresponding "mass increase" is quite significant. Instead of representing an increase of a few percent, it is a *factor of 7,000*. The new machines under consideration could increase that number to *50,000*.

These facilities will allow us to search for unknown particles in a new, and very large, energy region. There are several intriguing ideas about what could be found there – supersymmetric partners of known particles, Quantum Black Holes, other Higgs particles, evidence of extra dimensions, to name a few – but it is also possible that such a large unexplored region holds the great gift of new objects beyond our most daring theoretical speculations.

From faster computers to new perspectives

Undoubtedly, access to massive amounts of computing power, and the ability to successfully coordinate collaborations comprising thousands of researchers, has allowed us to probe intimate mechanisms of natural systems previously inaccessible, from the way fundamental interactions occur to finding our way through the myriad of connections in brain structures. Both enabling factors (computing power and collaboration tools) are actively being developed, and many efforts are under way to make data from large experiments available to the general public, to enable further enthusiasts and researchers to contribute to their study.

In parallel, developments in Artificial Intelligence and Machine Learning are being increasingly incorporated into the data-analysis toolbox of researchers in all disciplines. In particle physics, for example, the power of these techniques has forced their acceptance and use for particle identification, separation of signals and backgrounds in complicated searches, discriminating among suitable theoretical descriptions for a new phenomenon, etc.

Further into the future, there is also another possibility, both enticing and intriguing. Historically, some of the most fruitful developments in our understanding of nature have been made possible by detailed studies of the interfaces among different disciplines, and especially in areas with large discrepancies with experiment or glaring contradictions between theoretical descriptions. As the body of knowledge increases, so does the difficulty to understand two or more fields in such depth as to attempt such a new grand synthesis. The time needed to reach the current frontier of our knowledge keeps increasing, while our mental machinery does not. On the other hand, few doubt that we will develop, in the not-so-distant future, some form of Artificial General Intelligence (AGI's) which, once developed, will not be confined to the speed or capacity of their initial hardware implementation. After a few years, such systems may vastly surpass the human capacity to correlate information, find hidden patterns on experimental data and postulate theoretical models. Regardless of whether or not there is a limit to the human capacity to figure things out, one cannot help but wonder what new patterns, new insights, new math, new sciences, may be unveiled by our interaction and collaboration with such unprecedented information processing systems, either under our guidance... or not.

Keeping in touch

INVITATION TO CONNECT

For the latest news on Red Global MX Europe we invite you to follow our Facebook Page: www.rgmx.eu/fb

Email: contacto@rgmx.eu

Thank you!